VETERANS'
★DAY★

VETERANS' ★DAY★

By Douglas K. Pearson

Veterans' Day
© 2007 Douglas K. Pearson,
Storymakers, LLC

All rights reserved.

Edited by David Egner
Cover design by AUXILIARY Advertising & Design
Book design and layout: Dave Gilman

Printed in the United States of America
07 08 09 /TBD/ 10 9 8 7 6 5 4 3 2 1

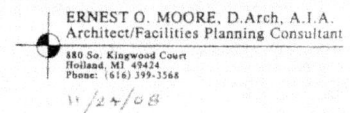

11/24/08

Dear Doug,

Please excuse my long delay in responding to the book "Veterans Day" that you gave me. My reading goes by fits and starts as I fit it in between lots of other activities. By the way it was a pleasure to meet you and to see your beautiful boat.

As for the impressions I had of the story in the book - I found it facinating and easy reading. I was a bit shocked at the violence that developed between the boys and the veterans. The treatment of the lad who was trapped in the one tank and the gun fire and flares aimed into the tank seemed excessive to me. I was a bit put off by part of that event. It was a facinating story however.

I like your story telling skills and thank you very much for sharing the story with me. Here is wishing you success!

Sincerely
Ernie Moore
WW II Veteran
Navy Combat aircrewman
Aviation mechanic
Retired Coast Guard Auxillary
Admiral in the Nebraska Navy
Avid sailor

Veterans' Day is dedicated to my late neighbor, Clarence Blakesly, whose appreciation for life not only sustained him as a frontline combat soldier in every battle in WWII except Normandy, but empowered him to continue freedom campaigns upon his arrival back home. Well into old age, he still liberated families in ways he only now understands. Especially mine. Readers would do well to find his book, A Personal Account of WWII by Draftee #35887149 and brand Clarence's worldview into their minds.

I also thank a teenage felon, Kyle Endicott. He's a small town Michigander kid who wrote a biography on fallen WWII veteran Frank Snarski. (Frank's name is engraved on a monument at the Veterans Memorial Park in Grand Rapids and was one of many defaced with fascist images.) Granted, young Kyle wrote this biography about Frank Snarski, after he got yelled at by Judge Dennis Leiber for vandalizing the sacred names. But readers would do well to see how Frank's surviving brother Joe modeled appreciation for life by agreeing to a mail interview to help young Kyle's research. Please view Kyle's PDF biography posted by the Grand Rapids Press:
http://blog.mlive.com/grpress/2008/08/SNARKI.pdf
or view it at my website http://douglaskpearson.com

Author's Note:

As shown by the book cover, Veterans' Day is about war and the subtle pulse within humanity that shatters dreams. As I venture you into this ocean (with some degree of concern), it is prudent to be aware that I borrowed some of Herman Melville's crayons. Especially the color white.

My story uses snow, television's white noise and some white people groups to reveal an organic oppression, as seen in the featured family and their inability to function on either side of the law.

The rotting white whale in Veterans' Day is the dysfunctional white elephant residing in a home that no longer wants to be ignored. As we take a good look at the trash of this family, let us be thankful for how they opened their story to show us why a human will lift a hand against another.

So when the Sherman Tank ca-chunks over the white picket fence, and its unblinking, star-shaped, zombie-dead-hungry white eye consumes its prey, be of courage dear reader, for the tank comes for us all. And it is a great, wonderful and liberating day when we come face to face with the white lie.

1
LEST WE FORGET

"Saying everybody's special is another way of saying nobody is."
—Dash Incredible

The thickly built teenager paused in the darkness then entered the ring of light on a snow-packed drive and stood in front of the weather-beaten, crusty building. High above him, ice clouds covered the black sky like worthless blankets. The young man had been cold for a long time. He kicked an ice chunk that clung to a pothole and spun it into the night.

From above the door, the dome light drone buzzed into his head and irritated him. White puffs of steam came from his mouth as he cursed Michigan, winter, the month of March and a few other cold things.

As if hearing him, an ice breeze slithered underneath his coat, curled around his neck and covered his body in chicken skin.

He tilted his head to read the three-lettered-sign, VFW. Beyond it, he saw the handicap ramp leading to a red, white and blue stripped door.

He spit.

The building stood still and cold like wind worn bones of something fragile and forgotten. Its windows a mere blink from surrender.

He wondered what VFW. stood for, so he took up an ice chunk and threw it at the sign to knock off the frost.

Sound sprang off into the night but ice still covered the fine print.

He knew old geezers came and went, so he took up another chunk of ice, threw it, and cracked open a window. Looking around for bigger ice, so he could take out another window, he frowned because they were all frozen into gravel in a way that would take much effort to break loose. He pocketed his short, chunky fingers, cursed the cold and used his short legs to motor his weeble-like body across the street and into his house.

> **post** *n.* 1 the place where a soldier, guard, etc. is stationed 2 a) a place where a body of troops is stationed; camp b) the troops at such a place; garrison 3 a local unit of a veterans' organization
> —*Webster's NewWorld Dictionary*

My name is Lefty. Lost my right arm to a Potato Masher at the end of the Great War. The Second Big One. World War Two. Bigger than all the squabbles in the last sixty years combined, even the ones the sniffling little toy soldiers cry about over at their memorials. Nam's their own fault.

If they'd have raised the flag over conquered ground instead of blowing the head off some tied up LBG (Little Brown Guy) in front of a news camera I might add, it might have helped their cause. Ahh, let 'em whine it!

Like we cared about memorials after our war! We were just glad the Croats didn't have the whole darn world speaking German! To be alive and have our country protected and in one piece was enough for us. Call me old-fashioned. Breathing American air is Jim Dandy handy!

I did stay in Europe a year or so after the war ended to decompress. Didn't have any family back home and didn't have the energy to make friends.

How could I?

And who can understand?

Who would want to?

No American civilian could that's for toot'n. Nor should they. Some levels of sinking are never meant to be. And World War is one of those things you don't want everybody digging too deep or else the entire population would be living out their slow days in Jitter Joints with fingers too jilted to hang onto a decent set of cards.

I looked at our V.F.W. ramp. It had useless and forgotten written all over it. I shuffled my sore feet up to our door and paused to catch my breath. But before I opened our red, white and blue door, I stopped, turned back and eyed the darkness. Tonguing my toothpick, I looked around.

The pitted road, hedged by gnarly trees didn't bother me. A stand of pines whispered harmlessly. The squatty houses to the east and south were asleep, but for the white vapor above their chimneys. One glowed blue from a TV.

I stepped inside but turned back to get a better look at that house to the east.

The one gnawing on the boob tube.

I wanted to see if that one was the one bothering me. But I didn't need proof. My long gone blown-up hand was stinging with shadow pain. Someone in there was watching me. Someone in the TV blue house.

I couldn't see him. Heck. I could barely see the house. But he was there alright.

2
THE WOUNDED

Splinter and Cell officially claimed the names, Slinter and Cell, when they bought Tom Clancy's Xbox™ game, Splinter Cell™. They then felt tougher. Splinter seemed to grow taller but less lanky as he cranked on a worn belt to keep his jeans above his narrow hips. He hated when his pants drooped because he didn't wear underwear. Crowded his style. Cramped his campers.

Splinter brushed some ganglily blond strands from his face, handed the lady a $50.00 and hoped she wouldn't steal his change. He grabbed the change from her and stuffed bills into his pocket before the numbers overloaded his brain.

He turned to Cell. "Let's do it!" Splinter said and twitched his shoulders under some shag.

Cell took the game and started reading the cover, veering right as he walked. He crunched into the line of shopping carts.

"Cell!" Splinter said.

Cell turned left without looking up. Being a gloppy boy, Cell had learned it was easier bounced off things than move around them. He had a good thick skin that held the body shape of a scuba suit bloated with water. Deep in his body was a skeleton but it didn't seem to have to work too hard from under the developing exoskeleton of heavy clothing, coats and his body armor. Cell wore a Kevlar vest that he got at the Army Surplus with his Christmas Cash. It helped him.

The two teenagers saw their reflection in the door and admired it. Cell's nose was kind of flattened to his face. Splinter's stuck out more like the beak on a small canine.

"Hold up the game." Splinter said.

Cell lifted it and they took it all in. They knew the game was the bridge. The medium. A conduit to another place and time.

They took another step into the world of modern warfare.

Splinter straightened his shoulders by bringing up his right. It had been slumping in its socket ever since grade school when he fired a turkey round from his dad's 12 gauge. His mom then sold that gun at a garage sale for $20 bucks. His dad left two weeks later.

Whatever. It didn't matter to Splinter. He had met Cell in the hospital recovery wing after the geeks relocated his shoulder.

Children's Protective Services or CPS made Cell go once every month for check-ups back then because his dad was a drinker. Cell's dad is long gone too.

Whatever. Doesn't matter to Cell.

The pair left the store and motored towards home in Splinter's '88 Ford Festiva.

Sinking on the passenger side because Cell, it puttered them along, over the pothole infested road towards Pocketville.

Like I said, I spent 1946 in the old country, wandering cobblestone roads through villages that predated cars. I went to the towns that we didn't bomb to rubble. Wherever I roamed, even in Switzerland, everybody knew me. I was an American G.I. My right sleeve flapping seemed to beckon people to shake my good hand.

Bakery owners came outside, broke open their warm bread and gave it to me just for walking by. Citizens bought me coffee. Café owners shared their local wines. Farmers filled my pockets with their cheeses. Children asked me for chewing gum.

People respected my soldiering. They knew I had given a piece of me to save their way of life. That year of meandering the countryside of Europe helped me find hope. And hope is hard to find and easy to lose when you're re-awakening up the part of your heart that you had to put to sleep to win the war.

Poker helps me now. Sounds stupid and you may laugh. But it ain't the game. It's the calm. And even though they call me Lefty, I hold my own with the two-handers.

They don't call me Lieutenant Ben Grumble of the 106th Combat Division. I don't refer to their past K Company's or M Company's either. We don't call each other Captains or Lieutenants because there's no rank among friends.

There are only five of us now. But we still gather every March at our VFW for the playoffs.

My four friends had arrived before me. They'll be a half hour early for their own funerals. It's not like they have anything else to do. We all have nothing else to do. But we do it anyways.

They're inside now and I'm still pausing at the door in the cold.

I'm eyeing that small, white blur of a house where the TV flickers blue in the windows. Or was it someone pushing aside a curtain? I trusted my shadow sting and lifted my left hand and gave a salute.

Curtains and widows remind me of a girl I knew 60 years ago.

I closed the door and walked the hallway of our VFW, frowning as I remembered the poker games of last year and how I lost some of my stuff. I squeezed feeling back into my hand. The arm I have goes numb and the one blown to pieces burns like blazes. Tell the little figurine to figure that!

I'm getting tired of my severed nerves stinging. Especially since my lost arm has been dust rot for some sixty years now. It happened near Evreaus, a town north of Paris.

I see French countryside in springtime.

I want to go back there and maybe a part of me has never left.

But it's just too close to Germany. That's where my only brother was killed in farmer's field above Saarbrucken. If I had stayed on in Europe I might start shooting all over again because I loved my brother. I probably would have been all right, but you never know. Nazis killed him with a Burp Gun. Bad sound. Bad times. Bad war.

I still hear his voice in my dreams. My mind can't let him go.

My family now are the veterans. The ones on down the VFW hallway.

I entered the room and saw them around the table. We are survivors. We've been family for over a half century. Our combat secrets keep us together. We know hell; it gnaws our souls and makes us old, nibbling away at our muscles and bones.

There are just five of us now and our chairs are getting bigger or we're withering. We're dying off at a regular pace. In four or five years we'll be all washed away just like our brothers on Normandy, Omaha and a good chunk of the Pacific beaches. I missed those battles because I entered the war a wet-behind-the-ears kid in

1944 and stayed alive by hanging onto bootstraps of old-timers as we pushed the Nazis across Europe, shredding every town, farm and living creature as we did so.

3

WAR GAMES

Officer Deep Pockets was on patrol when Splinter and Cell crossed into the city limits of Pockeville. Deep Pockets was the youngest and wisest of six Pocketville City Police officers and was a crack shot with the radar. He saw the Festiva, unslung the radar and thumbed the hammer for his flashers in one fluid, well oiled stroke. He soon leveraged the compact car to the shoulder as if it were on a leash. Deep Pockets walked up alongside and tapped on the driver-side window. It rolled down.

"License and Registration," he said, but then he pointed. "Pass me that."

Splinter and Cell looked at each other as fear settled into their loins as if they were losing balance near a cliff. Splinter's long ears seemed to fold against his neck as his military career faced a hiccup. Cell handed the game to Splinter. Splinter took a peaceful look at it and passed it out the window.

Deep Pockets took the game, turned it over and started reading the back cover. "This carries a 17 and older, M-Rating for Blood, Strong Language and Violence," he said.

"My mom got it for me," Splinter said.

"I wasn't asking a question. Stay in the car," Deep Pockets said and left, backing up to his squad car so no one could get the drop on him. He returned with the metal citation pad. "Do you have younger siblings at home?" he asked.

"No."

"Tell your mother she's very close to contributing," Deep Pockets handed back the game.

"Contributing to what?"

"To the delinquency of a minor," Deep Pockets said. "Why are you on this game any who? Is it because you don't have your whistle ready for the Xbox Live™! Hmm!" He clicked the pen. "Is this your current address? Or is your mom the queen of another double-wide trailer?"

Deep Pockets bent the driver's license then held it up to the bleak, Michigan sky and did a professional curt scan. Neatly dressed in blue uniform, his pants were bloused inside polished black combat boots. He was just another law enforcement agent in a snake infested Michigan winter wonder land.

"Is this your real age?" Deep Pockets was trying to separate the laminate.

"Do I look older?"

The officer spoke into his shoulder mic then scratched out the details of the citation.

Taking the ticket, Splinter looked out his car window at the officer's footwear. "Why do you tuck your pants into your boots?" he pointed to the officer's blousing.

"I can smell a cigarette if I want to. Do you want a full vehicle search? Do ya? You?" Deep Pockets asked, handing back the license.

Splinter shook his head, conceded and puttered away. He was followed through the rest of town but kept the speed limit. Splinter was a learning machine. Last month he got two citations in eight minutes from a Deep Pocket police officer. Like he was going to fall for that again.

Cell now held the game in both hands. That was close. They were at a blockade and couldn't prestige quicker without understanding the basic. Now he held the basic training game and felt its strong current.

They then set up Command Center at Splinter's house and were soon in combat zones of carnage. By the end of the day they were becoming soldiers anew. By the end of the week they had completed their re-training program and were again ready for prestige combat challenge. This time, they would do it with a knife! The real world of the X was calling to them. With the knife they would now kill military elite inside the Box!

After I lost two hands in a row, I went to the parking lot and scanned our trucks. We all still could drive you know, some better than others and I felt the urge to lock my truck. Then I grunted. None of us locked up our stuff.

Maybe we should start.

Why was I thinking this?

We all knew that the day we had to start locking up stuff meant the end was near. To lock up stuff raised the devil from the depths. Lucifer uses fear to suck the marrow out of bones and replace it with his cancer.

Locking doors made you old.

We didn't even lock the doors to the VFW until the Hippie Snippies came along. And then it was only because one of them did some hard time in a bamboo fish cage half under water. He felt safer when he was locked up.

My friend Beans said it made sense. Beans would know. He was in the Pacific Campaign and had stuff locked so tight in his heart that he forgot it was in a cage.

So we called a locksmith and installed a Schlage™ in 1972. Whatever it took to help a vet we'd all do.

I looked beyond our buzzing dome light. Squinting, I caught the flicker of blue glow in that house to the east. The house was as ugly as the woman who lived there with her little kid. I had seen her hoist her carcass out of her car once in a while. The dead blue hue was as much apart of the house as the exterior paint. She probably has blue lights in all her sockets to keep her insulated in case her plug-in-drug went on the blink.

I smirked and turned back to where the men were preparing cards.

Who was I to say how others should keep their sanity?

If she wanted a blue world let her have it. I lived in a red one most of the 1950's as I tried to blink away blood mist out of my mind. I incinerated some machine gunners into a red rainbow in '44. It took a good long time to see normal colors again.

I still don't like the color red. I can see it whenever I want. All I have to do is close my eyes.

Splinter and Cell met Red and Pal in Webworld after something akin to a Meet Your Combat Neighbor search in Modern Warfare™. They lived only ten miles apart. But fused by freedom's ring of gunfire the two groups formed a brotherhood closer than proximity. In the battles that followed, they became comrades. First through headgear. Then through practice.

They began training together in the same room. They traded in the headgear for more TV's. This level of soldiering equipped them to plan assaults and future sieges by day and launch insertions under the cover of darkness against various enemies foreign and abroad.

"It's happening, man!" Cell said. "We're getting pretty good."

"So what," Red said, dropping his controller into the lap of Pal. "It's like its not staying real for me."

"Really?" Cell asked, trying to be open to what was beyond his imagination.

"The plasma thing, man. I don't know. It's just not doing it for me today." Red stood and stretched.

Pal stood too. He handed the controller to the couch in a sacrilegious gesture.

Cell kept working the machine, leaning into the turns, one with the movement of the flanking unit.

Pal hit Red and nodded to the couch then pointed behind him.

Red walked back and closed the door.

"Splinter, dude, mind if I take a crack at your dog?"

"It's my mom's," Splinter said, not looking up from his screen.

Pal took aim, but waited until the canine looked at him.

Sprawled on the carpet by the heat vent, it had no fear of humans.

Pal aimed.

The dog blinked and a tail flickered.

The corner of Pal's mouth bent upward and he fired, yelping the dog and making it jump a few feet in the air.

"Stop it," Splinter said.

"Why?" Pal asked and took aim.

Now the dog was wary and eyed the weapon differently. Loosing the stare-down, it darted behind the chair going for cover.

But Pal was there against the wall, aiming the weapon steady at the pet.

"It's my mom's dog!" Splinter repeated from inside the zone.

Pal shot and the dog yelped and crossed the room in a bound, going for the door.

Red slammed it.

The dog stopped and pounced behind the footstool for cover.

"Dude!" Red said. "You see how quick that thing is?"

Pal went onto the floor, eye level with the dog and started stalking it from the far wall like a gilag suited sniper with a Berrat.

Ignoring all else, the dog eyed Pal from its shelter. It's upper lip curled and a snarl came forth.

Cell stopped playing and got killed.

Splinter's too.

Now they both became focused on a new war. One with a different reality factor.

Pal inched forward and the hair on the dog's neck stood. Eye to eye they tranced each other until the dog sprang backwards and bolted for the other door.

Red slammed it just in time, keeping the animal caged.

"Stop it!" Splinter said.

Pal stood, barrel down.

"Let me try," Splinter took the gun.

"The key is to go slow," Pal said. "Use the psychological factor. Freak it out and feel the terror."

Two hours later, Splinter's mom came back home from work and the door closed behind her. She saw her pet hiding behind a broom in the kitchen corner and it peed on the carpet. She took a step toward it and it just shook. A slushy turd drizzled from its butt as it tried to balance on four shaking legs.

She turned and walked into the living room and eyed the four boys arched around their four in-link TV screens. She commenced to end dog-hunting season there and then and threw the rocking chair through Splinter's TV.

Then she saw his Xbox™ and leaped forward to drive her heels through it. She was going for missile lock when Splinter dove on it.

Using his body as a shield, Splinter curled around it. He relied on his training.

Cell, Pal and Red saw the writing on the subway wall and got their systems while the woman put her boots to her son, making him yelp louder than the air-softed dog. But the three soldiers understood self-sacrifice. Inside their homes, they had at one time or another, risked life and limb to preserve their way of life from oppressive governments that wanted to trample the rights of the common man.

The got extracted from Splinter's house.

The four turned shoulder to the Michigan winter wind and looked at each other.

Splinter clutched his Xbox™, co-axel cables and connectors draped over his forearms and looked at the others doing likewise.

Pal and Red were mumbling about lost TVs.

"It'll still work on our TVs," Cell said. "They're just smaller."

"It'll just be more of the same crap," Red said.

"No it won't," Cell said. "My mom's too fat to go downstairs," Cell turned towards his house and the others fell in step.

It's hard to take the march out of the machine. Splinter brought up the rear, limping slow, war wounds from his old lady were giving him the shivers.

Back inside the VFW, I rubbed my chest with my hand and felt warmth. I smelled dust and mildew in the air. Our furnace seemed to be burning cooler. I made it down the hallway, by the black and white pictures and some belts of 50 caliber duds. I entered the card room and Ned pushed out a chair for me as if I needed the help. We glared at each other awhile then nodded.

It would take a lot more than sympathy to turn my resolve. The month of March had begun. The greatest time in the entire year. March was the month we learned that Adolph, pride of the fascists faggots of the world, froze his entire northern army on the Russian Front. Poor Adolph and his quarter million pets. Once God iced over the Laptiv Sea, there was nothing to warm those Artic Winds except all those poorly dressed Nazis. Good thing Adolph was no weatherman.

March is the greatest month of the near.

March turned the tide.

I felt my luck changing now too. I looked around at the faces of my friends. I saw the uncut deck of cards and sat in my spot. A year had passed and now things were coming to boil.

I looked at Beans and then at the table next to his belly. He lifted his hand and I saw the gold nuggets. He had dozens of them and his fingers scooped and dropped them back on the table over and again. Dull thuds of heavy metal called to me.

"Getting ready to say goodbye to my gold?" I asked.

Beans grunted.

I looked in his eyes. "You should. I see you're keeping 'em nice and shiny. Mine are mine!"

Bean grunted. Expected.

I looked back at the glowing nuggets. They were mine. The whole table knew the 29 gold teeth were mine. I was the one who rifle-butted them out of the jaws of a of bunch of dead Nazis. I looked back at Beans, pulled out a Lugar, put it on the table and spun it with my fingers.

Everyone around me leaned in and knew I meant business. They each dropped a palm over their teeth, favoring the ones that they had claimed themselves.

Beans eyed the pistol and let the gold teeth drop and cupped them with his fingers. He then knew I had come to re-take ground.

We all knew Beans would bet the farm and all its critters to get his hands on Nazi weapons.

4
RAID

It was nearing midnight when Splinter took up his coat to leave Cell's house. His mom held him to a midnight curfew because she wanted him to get decent rest on school nights.

"Where you going?" Red asked.

"Home."

"Yelpy! Yelpy!" Pal said.

Splinter shrugged on coats, turned from the screens and blinked his eyes back into shape.

"Nail the VFW for us," Cell said.

"Okay."

Turning shoulder to the cold, Splinter stepped into the night. He inhaled frigid air around his tongue to warm it before it came into his lungs and saw white fog steam from his nostrils as he exhaled. Lone snowflakes floated through the air like silent white bugs. Ice crunched as he walked toward the buzzing farm light beyond the four corners. Once there, he stopped. Around him was a sea of gray snow. He saw no headlights. Icy branches ticked into one another and snapped as they adjusted to the night frost.

Splinter drew his phone, punched a number and put it to his ear. "What's VFW stand for?" Splinter asked Cell.

"What are you? Stupid?" Cell asked.

"You don't know either, do you?"

"So. At least I'm not stupid. Ask your dog, Barfy Boner! You do a window yet?" Cell asked.

"No. There's trucks over here!" Splinter said. There was a silence. He stood on the road in front of the faded, sign. "It says, Veterans of Foreign Wars. Are the guys in there really soldiers?"

"No. And no one's ever there," Cell said.

"Ask Red," Splinter said.

"Why?"

"Lights are on."

"Really?"

"Ya." Splinter said. "And I'm still gonna bust out a window!"

"Cool," Cell said. There was a pause. "Wait for the support!"

Splinter pocketed his phone and kept eyeing the place as his friends piled into Red's truck harrier up behind him. He looked at his feet and picked up some chunks of asphalt that the road excreted this time of year.

"Soldier this!" Splinter said and loaded his ammo into the bed of Red's truck with Cell and Pal.

Now I'm in my late 80's and the youngest and ablest of the crowd despite missing an arm. I guess that's why my name came up after the window above our card table shattered, spraying glass onto our heads. I moved my eyes from left to right and saw how Wendell, Ned, Beans, Webb and probably myself were all starting look more alike than ever because our skulls were coming through our faces.

We looked around the room, saw the rock and then back up at the window.

"You gonna fix that, Lefty?" Beans asked, "Or you gonna sit there and whiffle your sniffle?" The cheeks of Beans flushing red in anger. That wasn't good.

Like I said, Beans was in the Pacific Campaign. He could tell stories that could spoil a jar of pickles. One of his stories wrecked out 1971 for me. The whole year! Beans had areas of his soul still churning up stuff and sometimes he's gotta spill it. That's how he got his name.

It wasn't until but thirty years ago when we learned that Beans had it worse than the ordinary tortured soldier. We should have figured that out earlier. Heck. He didn't even speak to us from 1947 to 1962. Not a word for fifteen years!

Beans not only didn't talk about the war, he didn't talk.

We think there's a part of Beans that's missing, something deep down in his innards where normal people have a soul.

I think a part of Beans has stopped living altogether. And when someone becomes more than 51% Zombie, it makes a person a little unstable in the dangerous sort of way. Not that he looks all that ordinary.

Bean's body is all but 120 pounds. Soaking wet. But his eyes can ignite a green tree stump.

I think it's the deadness to both fear and life that has kept Beans above ground. Then and now. To each his own. And the story he did tell once, I wish it had never been spoken of. After Beans left that day the rest of us swore an oath never to repeat it. Some things about the rot of human nature shouldn't be said. Not ever. And some things spoken of in the South Pacific, nobody would believe anyways.

But we do. And we know the truth about Beans.

He has more stories. Worse ones than that. One's we hope he'll never spill. Evil happenings that should go grave out of kindness to humanity.

We all looked at each other as the cold poured down on us from the open window.

It was time to ante up.

Now we have all eaten enough Spam to not slam our tally's in the tailgate by having some glass tinkle around us. A few years ago it might have been different, you know, with the war hating hippies around. They sure were a lost bunch. But March is our month and we got the place to ourselves. And now we're just tired. Even the hippies are tired. We've been around a long time.

"No." Webb said. I knew Webb would say no. It's been in his eyes since he slipped on ice back in 1984. "Let it be. Let it go. Especially you, Beans," Webb said.

Cards were on the table and Webb, low on teeth himself for the last decade, added a Nazi medal to the pot. For Webb not to fold took quite a hand. No wonder he didn't care about the broken window.

"Let what go?" Beans asked. "It's gett'n cold. Why play cards in the cold?"

I looked at the hole in the window above our walnut card table. The table was cold but that wasn't Beans's point. Wasn't his point at all.

We all knew Bean's had Malaria some seventeen times so he probably couldn't get cold if he spent Easter swimming in Lake Michigan.

I pulled my hand off the table and drew my cards to my chest. It was getting cold. Those big severed nerves under my right nub get chilly real quick.

"Stuff it, Lefty!" Ned said. He had authority, being the only one with hair. He nodded at me. Ned could still see a fly on the wall too.

But not seeing bugs was a fringe benefit of being half senile to me. But I can see them when I close my eyes. I see them feasting on the juicy faces of the dead. I put down my cards and got up.

"Let it be." Webb said. Webb was small and short and in denial that his barrel chest had eroded away.

Being a helmet head, I kept going. I took a dusty blanket from the mildew couch, twisted one end and plugged the hole in the window, minding the cracks. Then I sat and took up my cards, knowing that the sound of breaking glass can awaken things that should stay asleep. And then it happened.

The blanket blew back into our place and another big ole rock thunked our table, rattled the gold teeth and some other treasures before spinning out across our floor. I saw Webb's cards.

He was holding hearts. Lots of them.

The last piece of glass stopped dancing on the floor.

Wendell stood first. He had good lift because he bought new knees back in the '90s at a two for one sale from a hospital in Wichita. Wendell was short too and that always helps a man keep his girth. He still had some muscle and fat where the rest of us were more like the skin and bone handiwork of the Bat Jap Rat Camps. Gravity stuck the rest of us to our chairs like pin-pierced bugs in some kid's collection.

"Bones and witches!" Wendell said under breath, shuffling to the door. He opened it and yelled, "Bones and witches!" into the night.

We listened from our poker table. We heard them laughing at us.

They were in our parking lot. Their small little headlamps cut the darkness and tried to flood the room with some light as the motor roared.

We heard the gravel and ice, being slung by their spinning tires, bounce off our post and pickups as their truck circled. Some peanut size stones rolled on into our post and down the hallway only to fizzle out and stop on the tile by our feet.

"That's a hurting V-8," Webb said as he popped a piece of splintered glass from where it stuck in our table next to his cards.

"Yell it again!" Beans said. He was standing now next to Wendell at the door.

Wendell did, shaking a fist. Wendell was a cusser when he got going.

When the snow dust cleared, Wendell found himself venturing under the glow of the buzzing light above our red, white and blue front door.

None of the rest of us went out into the open. But it wasn't because the cold or that we wanted to stay warm. We had all gotten up only to slink against the walls and behind some door frames. Some habits should be broken, but none of us were ever very good at that.

Beans flipped the switch and the light outside went dead. We then stepped out into the open and the night. Our eyes adjusted to the darkness and we pointed out some dings and dongs to Webb's truck which was closest to where the weasels carved their little ditches in our frozen dirt.

They messed up our dirt.

Back inside, I stuffed the window again and we took up our cards. I bumped the light above the table and it swung, throwing shadow. I looked at the faces of my friends and I felt a sadness coming over us. I got to thinking about Webb's cards. Those hearts were stacked nice and neat, face down in front of him. For him not to touch a good hand meant something.

"What's wrong with you?" Ned asked Webb. Webb had his reading glasses off and a white handkerchief was still against his eye. He pulled it away and we saw red. Glow red.

"Shrapnel got me from the window," Webb said.

We took his body to steady it, brushed cards and teeth off the table and laid him on top.

Webb's cards landed face up on some gold. He had a flush. It would have been tough to beat.

"I guess you didn't see much when you went outside." Bean's said.

"What do you want?" Anyone of us could have asked it. Anyone of us would do whatever a wounded man wished.

Honor was our way.

Webb swore at the pain and that was saying a lot because he was a God-fearing Baptist. "Hold the light still!" Webb said. "When it swings it's like I'm back on the boat."

I stopped the swinging light with my hand.

Webb hates boats. Even in his peak angling days he only fished from shore. Some soldiers who survived Normandy hate boats. In fact they hate anything that can sink because it gives them jitters.

Beans is not as bad as Webb. In the Pacific they got the feel of storming a beach. In a sea of blood they surfed in on the carcasses of the dead, using the fallen to hide and shield them in the waves. Ebb and flow. Watch the documentaries and be thankful they are in black and white.

We pulled the rag away and held his eye still with our fingers.

"You see anything?" Webb asked.

We all leaned forward.

"Yes," Ned said. "I see it." Ned could still see, as I mentioned before and pointed to blood oozing from the soft white tissue of Webb's eyeball. Ned pulled out a warm Leatherman™ from his pocket with his free hand. Webb liked to keep stuff in his pockets. He still carries around a silver dollar so he'd never be broke. It's as thin as tin foil. He boasted that he could bend it just by looking at it. He touches it whenever he holds a full house or better. We'd all fold if it ever clinked across our table. It would mean a Royal Flush!

"I gave up doctoring 20 years ago," Ned said. "I might not get it the first time."

"Shut up and yank it!" Webb swore. Ned opened the pliers, leaned in and took hold of his friend's face with his free hand. But the hand that held the tool did shake some.

I looked at Beans.

Bean's saw it too.

I tugged at the biggest sagging flap on my neck like I did after a hand of bad cards.

Ned swung the needle nose pliers over to Beans who had taken out his lighter. They cooked off the bad germs. Old habit. Proven ways. Ain't broke and don't fix it.

Wendell, seeing blood and fire, stepped back and walked away. His eyes glassed over and he took hold of the cold tabletop to steady himself. His other hand touched his leg. That wasn't a good sign. He did it before he folded.

"Rest your palm on his cheek, Ned. It'll steady your hand," Beans said, still panting from walking back from the parking lot.

Ned did so and soon plucked something from Webb's eye socket and held it up to the light.

Webb sat up and looked around blinking.

"I don't see anything," I said. "You sure you got it?"

"I got the pot-licker," Ned said. "First time too."

"Lemme see," Webb said, taking hold of the tool and trying to see it. "Is it there?"

"It's there," Ned said. "It looks like red thread."

"No wonder I can't see it. I haven't seen thread since the 60's," Webb said.

"Bones and witches!" Wendell said, coming back. He rubbed his scar that covered an empty spot on his thigh that was missing half its steak. Then he brushed glass off the table, knelt and started picking up stuff.

We looked at the broken window of our VFW Hall. I went stuffed it again. I used a pillow this time.

Beans came up off his knees with the cards and teeth and we reset and dealt a new hand.

"I had a flush as sweet as those French women," Webb said.

As if I didn't know.

We all went quiet.

Nice thing about those French women. They never got any older, which is a polite way to say a lot of things. I wondered if they still thought the same about us. Back then we all had the same haircut, uniform and mannerisms. Back then we were all the same too. Those French woman would be the first to admit that.

A mile away inside the deserted pole barn, Cell added another log to the smoking fire in a burn-barrel and held out his hands, hoping for heat. He looked around at the faces of his friends, partially hidden in shadow. "Did you see them?" Cell asked. "I saw them!"

Pal pulled a burning twig from the fire and held it to his cigarette. "They're there alright. Wonder why?"

"What'll they do?" Splinter asked.

"Dunno," Pal said. "They can barely walk whoever they are."

"My Grandpa can still walk! We're morons," Red said.

"Morons?"

"Moron or not he can still walk. And drive!" Red said.

Splinter's face glowed blank in the firelight.

Pal dragged his smoke and looked into the night. "Then they're kin," Pal said. "Your Grandpa and those geezers are kin. They're brotherhood."

"So," Splinter said.

"Yea! So what?" Cell said.

"It's true then." Pal said and they all looked at Red.

Red looked up from the fire. "It's just like any other mission," Red said. "We better not get captured alive."

5
High School Lecture

As tradition, Ned, whose real name was Dr. Allen Mitchell, spoke to the U.S. Government class before Spring Break. That's when Pocketville High School used their prime learning time to spend a few days teaching WWII.

Students knew Ned as Captain Mitchell and townsfolk just called him Cap'n whenever he was seen around Pocketville, despite the fact that he corrected them all the time because he left the military as a low ranking Corporal. Maybe the mix-up came because both words started with the letter C. Or maybe it was because Ned looked and acted like a Captain. He could command people.

As Ned made the long march to his class, the student aide guiding him stopped and paused every minute or so, so Ned could catch up.

Ned felt like complaining but knew that Beans had survived Bataan, not that anyone around here would be able to teach that. It's not popular to teach truths that are scarier than fiction. He stopped again for breath and acted like his cane needed adjusting.

The day had come when a little girl could out march him. Hells Bells!

"The bell's going to ring soon," she said.

He knew the drill. The natives went crazy between classes. Ned hated being with the peasants. He called them Village People, but he also saw answering questions on WWII as a civic duty that trumped his biases. Kind of like walking in the Fourth of July Parade. A lot of hassle and sweat until a child asked the parent, "Why?"

Only now most parents seem to point at the fire trucks and the candy instead of the soldiers.

Ned made it to the auditorium and entered.

A few years ago they started combining all the Government students when he spoke. That way Ned didn't have to say the same thing four times and run out of patience. That's what the teacher had said.

Ned entered the large, quiet hall and climbed the four big steps to the stage and traded handshakes with the fudgy, plump teacher.

They sat behind a microphone on a stage with two chairs. Then the bell rang and the ants came marching in. Noise grew for five minutes and peaked just after the second bell.

The teacher turned to Captain Mitchell. "Thanks for doing this, Cap'n," he said. The man had learned years ago to say that before the soldier spoke, establishing a plausible deniability for the parent phone calls after Ned gave a soldier's perspective on something or another.

The teacher looked at the dark, waxy paper sack resting in Ned's lap. "Anything special planned?" the man asked.

"That kind of depends on the questions, doesn't it?" Ned said.

"Yea. I guess," the teacher said. "But I got ask you this anyways. You don't have any guns in the sack do you? School systems won't stand for any guns anymore. Different times. Changed ways."

"No guns," Ned said. "We're not at war." Ned looked at the crowd. A couple of grenades would do the trick.

With the stadium seating filled with nearly 100 students, the teacher stood, checked the microphone and introduced Captain Mitchell. He spoke of the soldier's years of service, outlined his role in a few battles and talked of the machinery he worked on. The teacher used a video projector interfaced with the Internet and had a student show pictures supporting Captain Mitchell's experience with the Sherman Tank, M-9 Machine Carbine as well as satellite photographs of the locations of battles and statistics. Then he motioned for Captain Mitchell to come forward.

Students applauded.

Ned caught his focus. Seeing the picture from the projector was new this year. It took him back a ways. He cleared his throat.

"Can you find a picture of a German Panzer Tank?" Ned asked the big screen as if it were a voice activated computer.

Up in the sound booth, a geek clicked the screen to a Google Search and soon blinked the screen to a Panzer tank. Dirty and stark. Gritty and seasoned it made Ned lose his thought for a moment. Panzer's were built to kill the world's men.

Ned cleared his throat and leaned to the microphone. "Like much of the war, the tide turned because Hitler made a few seemingly harmless decisions that fell in the Allies favor. I know that because there are still people around. People speaking languages other than German. Hitler's pride halted the building of these Panzers in '43 because he favored the bigger Elephant Tank. It took at least four of our Shermans to kill a Panzer. Panzers were faster with quicker turrets and better guns. They killed us like fish in a barrel." A murmuring rose and Cap'n looked at the teacher. "Any questions?" Cap'n asked.

A boy raised his hand.

"Stand." Captain said.

The boy did."You ever kill anyone, Cap'n?" the boy asked.

Ned looked at the kid. The boy wasn't wearing black or fancying a tattoo. Nothing was stabbed though his nose or lips. His hair wasn't neon or in a Mohawk. He didn't have hippie biker hair below his shoulders. It wasn't the old days anymore. These were the new and improved days. Ned missed those old days. Back in those days there were only a few scum.

Ned looked out over the crowd. Since when did clean cut boys become scum? Little disrespectful pieces of scum that don't know nothing about nothing! Maybe Beans and Wendell were right. Maybe the five of them were just too old to influence anything anymore. Maybe the days of duty were done. It was time for him to retire. He looked at exit sign at the back of the auditorium. He was drawn to it and felt himself leaning. But even the sign seemed too far away.

Instead, Ned pointed his finger at the boy again as other students quickly raised their hands. Ned knew the drill. They wanted bloodsport. He pointed at the boy who asked the first question and was still raising his hand for a follow-up. Ned motioned him forward with his finger.

"What?" the boy asked.

"Come."

"Where?"

"Up here," Ned said.

"I just wanted to ask you how many?" the boy said.

There used to be none who would ask this. Then a few. Now they all wanted to dance with the details of death. Ned looked at the teacher until the man lowered his eyes. It had been nearly sixty years since that war. No one asked Ned questions like this during the first thirty. But those decades were done and gone.

"It's been sixty years," Cap'n said.

"You forget how many?" the boy asked, climbing the steps to the stage and standing awkward, unaware that he interrupted Ned.

"No," Cap'n spoke and fire was in his eyes and the boy hesitated to go closer. "You forgot, son. You and all your witches have forgotten." He waved the cane like the staff of Moses, then pointed at the girl who was sitting in the chair next to the one vacated by the boy. He knew they were a Jack and Jill.

"What?" the girl asked.

"Come on up here and stand by your pony," Ned said.

She came up.

"At least you two haven't forgotten anything important. That's the good news. The bad news is that you never learned anything important in the first place!" Ned could have gored his cane through the cowardly boy and wiped off the blood on sweater of the sweetheart. Instead, he looked back at the crowd and shook his head, ashamed to be their speaker. Maybe Beans was getting to him. Maybe his energy was dry.

"What are you talking about?" the girl on stage said. She saw the old man's body shaking. She reached to steady him. A gesture of maternal in a age of declining growth rates.

Ned stopped shaking and the two students stood there next to him. Even the girl was taller than the veteran soldier.

Captain gripped his paper bag and felt better. He looked at the crowd, "Now pay attention because I'm old and tired. Have I ever killed a man? Well, yes. I have. His name was Bronx and he was young and dumb like these two. But he was smart. Smart enough to know that I knew how to stay alive."

Captain then grabbed the boy's right wrist, turned and dropped the boys hand to his left hip. "Grab my belt." Ned said.

The boy blushed. The crowd laughed because Ned said the word, belt.

"You asked the question now dance to the answer. Grab the belt if you want to know."

"Grab it!" someone yelled out.

The boy took hold of the Captain's belt. He made a fist around it.

Captain brought the microphone up. "Hold my belt when the 88's come! I told Bronx. We were going against a German tank division that was dug in and they had a good flank of mortars. We were jumping from fox hole to hole as the bombs whistled down. We were Recon."

Ned spoke to the two on stage, ignoring the audience, who were giggling once in a while at their friends. But he kept his mouth to the microphone. "After the 88's cut our division apart I found the kid. The one we called Bronx. He'd been cut in two. His armless torso was under the mud but he was still alive when I pulled him out. He wasn't bleeding out because his innards were cauterized. I wiped the mud off his face and he saw the truth. He then wanted me to kill him. He was in agony. His arms were gone otherwise he'd have done it himself."

Students stopped laughing. They were looking around. Was Cap'n using hyperbole?

"So I drew my .45 and shot my friend, Bronx. I blew the back of his head off. Most of it went into the dirt but some bone and brain blew back my way and stuck to my arm and face. You know, normal killing stuff. Bronx had that organic smell of live blood. I saw my .45 and my arm glow red with his life blood."

Ned looked at the boy still holding his belt, Captain's left hand had clamped on the boy's hand, fastening it to his belt. Ned then reached into a paper bag. His right pulled out a yellowed, leathery stick thing.

"The fire fight hit us hard about then and I had to scramble," Ned said, seeing the students listening. "Those mortars kept us jumping around for a couple of hours. Later that night, I reached behind me and found out that this was still attached to my belt. I'd been diving from fox hole to hole for hours but it was still there."

He held it up. "Bronx's arm," he said cold and flat. "Look close at the arm of my friend, Bronx!"

It went still and quiet.

Students then saw the yellow ulna bone protruding because the leather had shrank. Ned looked at the boy, whose face was going white. The girl was stepping away. Cap'n lifted the arm to the boy. "I keep this so I never forget that I killed a person."

For a moment the boy thought Captain Mitchell was going to hand the arm to him. He didn't know if he should take it. He let go of the man's belt.

The teenager never saw the blur.

Bronx's bone and hard leather was like a club. It knocked the boy sideways into the girl and they both tumbled clean off the stage and landed in a heap. Students stopped giggling for the first time. "I'm Corporal Ned Mitchell! Anymore of you giggling Bam Bam's and bimbos care to shake hands with one of my friends? One of the human beings that I killed?"

All was quiet.

"What? No more stories on death? No more jokes on killing? Funny times over all of a sudden? Okay then. Here's what you need to know about World War Two. It was World War Two! The world was at war! People had forgotten that evil exist. Ten percent of the world got themselves killed! Ninety percent of the world went hungry and suffered the wrath of diseases for a few decades." Ned looked around.

The teacher was looking at the floor, rubbing his temples. He knew learning was happening despite being at school. But now was not the time. Now his work was just starting. He could already hear the phone ringing.

The couple who had gotten knocked off the staged had untangled themselves.

"There's more!" Ned said. "Evil still exists. Billions have forgotten. Billions will die. Don't get too attached to your kids if your generation ever figures out how to have them! Take a lot of pictures of them while they're young. Wars like that come around every century or so. When you send them off? They won't come back!"

Ned turned to the boy on the floor now holding his jaw. A trickle of blood was running down his chin. Their eyes met and Ned dropped Bronx's arm down onto the pair.

They slid back as if it were a snake.

Ned pointed at them. "You two go and take Bronx's arm. You paid for it with your insolence. Keep it on the shelf in your classroom where you can take it down and dust it off when little kids start doing stupid things. Things like vandalism and disrespecting soldiers and their memories." Ned looked at crowd, then at the teacher.

The teacher's face faded another shade of white and the expression promised nothing.

Ned didn't care; he had seen the cartoon pictures in the textbook. He caned himself down the stairs and shuffled up the carpet between the silent hordes and walked out the door.

In the empty corridors, he went to the wall and leaned against it. Fumbling out a white handkerchief, he wiped sweat off his brow until the jitters passed. Alone, he caned his way to the parking lot and lifted his collar to the frosty wind-chill. He looked for the sun in the all white sky, but no area was brighter than the other. He had a strange feeling in his stomach.

Ned felt good.

Snowmelt pooled at their feet as the four teenagers sat and took off layers and compared paintball body welts.

"Summer ones are better," Cell said. "They turn color quicker."

"It's the cold that keeps the swelling down," Splinter said.

Red dropped his gun on the sofa, stepping over slush and exhaled hard. "You'd be lucky to walk away from those on a summer day," he pointed a three red circles on Cell arm from his automatic burst. "Man at that range you'd be toast."

"Not anymore," Cell said. "It just doesn't hurt anymore. It's happening."

"No it's not," Pal said. "Nothing's happening and quick."

"What's wrong?" Red asked Pal. "You sore cause you keep missing or keep getting shot?"

"You wanna know? I'll tell you," Pal said. "At the end of the day it's still just a game. Everything is just a game! Just for giggles and squirts. Just for fun. It's hard for me. I feel like I'm wired for war."

Pal and Red looked at each other.

"Follow me," Pal said and stepped back in his boots. He took up his air rifle and went up the steps and outside.

Cold rippled his skin and he felt the sweat along his body cool to near frost on his back. He looked at the others and saw steam come off their bodies.

Cell shuddered then embraced the cold.

They walked across the property to a stand of trees, and Pal stopped.

"What are you doing?" Cell asked.

"Watch this!" Pal pointed. All was quiet and still, except for a few passing cars.

They looked through the pine trees and across the road to the VFW then back at Pal, who was aiming at Cell's house.

He nestled against a tree. White steam swirled from his nostrils as his still body embraced the cold, slowing itself down to focus his aim. His finger squeezed the trigger and the rifle leaped in his arms. As it settled, other rounds were fired. Across the way, two eyes, one nose and a pretty descent smile appeared side of the house.

Then the others stepped forward, leaned against trees and joined Pal. The home was only hundred feet away. They were kitty corner to it.

"I can't make a face," Cell said.

"I know," Pall said, keeping his shoulder against a tree to steady more of his shots. "How could you? It takes a good weapon. It takes practice."

6

Attack

It was a rare day. Not only was the sun out, it was bright. We all had to squint.

Especially Webb. His eye had stayed stiff and sore despite the temperature rise. He couldn't even take off his thick black glasses that covered his seeing glasses.

But our lungs were filled with the hope of spring and all was healing. The season of cloud and cold had broke and we busied ourselves around our turf that Saturday morning. More than ice was melting this day.

Us five worked as a team again. Or tried to anyway. All most of us could do was watch the snow melt to mud around our dull, white VFW Post 3946. Whenever the frost came out of the ground, our small, dungy concrete structure seemed to sink into the muck like the Half Tracks in the bogs of bygone Europe.

Webb brought out his toys and grated away brown puddles in our parking lot with his restored '38 John Deere. He dragged the oozing ice muck out onto the road. Snow melt had a good flow next to the roadway and the merging of clear and mud waters looked like Yukon glacier muck river merging with the crystal clear Klondike.

Webb liked his stuff, especially his pre WWII tractors. They were made when men worked the factories. When real men built stuff for real men to use and maintain. They were created in an era when nothing was disposable.

We were watching Webb when he idled the tractor down and pointed at a Pocketville police cruiser which had slowed and turned into our driveway.

The black and white stopped next to the tractor. Webb let the engine idle a bit longer than necessary, then shut it off and got down.

Me, Beans, Ned and Wendell found ourselves leaning on our heavy rakes.

Webb walked away from the officer's car and stood by us.

The passenger side window of the police car went down. "Afternoon men," the officer called out. "You men obtain your grating permit this year?"

"We're not grating," Webb said. "We're still plowing snow. We don't need no silt fence"

Now having the boy's in blue sniff around for handouts was nothing new. They always seemed to smell us out whenever we grated away the goosh from the gravel and sent it downstream with the winter melt. They always argue that it can't go into the river that cuts Pocketville in two.

I looked to the road. The asphalt was layered deep with our piled mud which spawned a brown river as far as I could see.

The officer stepped out of his patrol car and we watched his shiny boots sink into the fresh grated mud. His face flushed, but after closer inspection it just looked tan, like he slept under one of those therapy lights that Webb's wife uses to combat SAD or Seasonal Affective Disorder.

"There's plenty of ice in that dirt," Webb said, pointing to the road heap. "She'll just melt away."

The officer sank another foot in the mud and looked back at the clean interior of his car.

We all remembered what The City told us at last year's Fall Festival. How they had put us on their Environmental Watch List and that they'd keep calling on us. At least they were honest about that.

"The riverbed is already filled with dirt," Beans said. "So's the planet for that matter!" He turned his back on the officer and looked at Ned. "If he wants to see environmental damage he should have seen what we did in the Pacific. Those places still aren't normal."

The policeman walked forward. "We have city trucks out repairing plow scars and they said you men were up to your old tricks," he said.

"You and the mayor's yard boys don't need to be afraid of us. We're just plowing some snow," Webb said.

We let Webb talk.

Webb always paid the citations. They were cheaper and easier than putting up a silt fence to slow mudflow.

For the rest of us, it was another yearly tax. We put the tickets in frames above our card table. Whenever we get drunk and cynical, we point to them and thank our buddies who got blown to bits so America could be free.

"You know we'll just pay it. So of course you're gonna keep coming!" Beans said. "We're just the fiddle tappers. You're the rat, toot'n the fascist horn!"

"No need to get snippy, Captain," the officer said.

I could tell he didn't like Beans. No surprise there. It took me fifty five years of practicing kindness to Beans before he gave me the time of day. And now that he had my little gold nuggets, he was getting cockier by the moment.

"What we're trying to say is," Ned said, "Is that soldiers aren't the one's who think a ticket writing pen is mightier than a sword. You might want to think about that, when you wash the salt off your little white car!"

The officer approached us, showing off his mustard by walking through a mud puddle. His black books sunk deep into some soft spots but his pants stayed clean, bloused into his boots the way they were. He was going to have to walk through a lot more than mud if he wanted to look us in the eye if you know what I mean.

"You men are being obstinate," the officer lifted his metal citation pad, "This here's the basic citation we give to all developers this time of year when they fill our city sewers up with sludge. It's nothing personal."

"So they're your city sewers?" Beans asked. "You live in them?"

The man wrote the ticket and gave it to Webb.

"Thank you," Webb said and the officer lifted his boot and looked at the mud underneath.

"You should bring in some gravel. Then you won't have to grate every spring?" he looked over at the oozing mud that Webb had piled near the road. "You make it hard for us to come out here and do this."

"It's also hard when the little Bingo Girls cry when they get mud on their glass slippers," Webb said.

"I don't think you know the first thing about getting hard," Beans said.

"We almost got 'er done," I said, seeing Webb starting to boil. "Think she'll be a nice spring?"

"Are those glass slippers?" Beans asked, pointing down at the officer's boots.

"I'm ready for summer," the officer said. "Less hassle when driving conditions improve." He closed his metal citation pad. He then stepped through the mud and back into his cruiser.

"Good-bye Cinderella," Beans said to him.

The officer held his finger on the button and the window went up and he drove off.

Ned and Wendell came alongside and the five of us were together when it happened.

We were hoping to work the grounds. To do some good manly work. Get some fresh air. Maybe a blister. Do a job that had closure and allowed us to talk about man stuff around the poker table at night. Do something to steady the jitters and end the day without feeling emasculated by a culture that pushed us out of the workforce.

But it happened nevertheless. The air started whistling. The sound scared us. It all came back.

Impacts thudded our post.

"Incoming," Beans said in his same voice he used when asking for more coffee.

We found ourselves behind the big rock under the flag. A big rock is some pretty descent cover. Then it was quiet again, but only for a second.

"What is that?" Ned asked. He pointed at some color spots running down the white walls of our post.

Beans did a quick scan of the surroundings. He seemed to know something.

The rest of us just looked at the paint spots. Then all went still. We waited a minute or so then crept into the open.

"They came from those blue spruces," Ned said.

I saw a blob of green trees as well as a patch of brown that was the field alongside it. But I hadn't been able to see trees in forest since the 80's.

We waited out their by our rock. Minutes passed. None of us were in the mood to step into the open. We took turns looking up at the flag against blue sky.

It's brass clips echoed the hollow aluminum post.

We were getting shot at under the banner of red, white and blue once again.

"Turn on the hose, Lefty," Webb said.

I walked into the open, amazed that the feeling of not caring about getting shot came upon me. You don't forget how to ride a bike.

Beans went into the open next. "Whatta you see, Ned?" he said as he helped drag the heavy black hose across the mud. Beans turned the nozzle at the end and sprayed the wall, leaning into the hose as if was his old, Jap-cooking flame-thrower.

Ned, Webb, Wendell and I became leery of open spaces. We started distancing ourselves from each other.

Beans hosed.

Ned watched the trees.

The rest of us fanned out and looked at the color on our walls.

"It's paint," Wendell called out. "Bones and witches. My great grandkids have those! They're toys." He reached up and wiped off an orange paint splat. "It's from a paintball gun."

"Since when is a gun a toy?" Webb asked.

I walked up and touched it. "Yup," I said. "It's paint. Water soluble. What's it from?"

"A paintball gun." Wendell said as if I was stupid. "They shoot these little marble sized bullets filled with paint."

I turned and looked at the green of blue spruces across the way. It was a ways away. "What's the range?" I asked, but no one heard.

"Blast it again, Beans," Webb said.

Beans did, leveling the stream like a man used to burning soldiers out of caves. "We just going to wash it off?" Beans asked, looking away from the wall and trying to see where it came from. Then he pointed at another dozen or so green, blue, red and orange splats. "We just gonna wash it off like nothing's happening here?"

"They're from a paintball toy," Wendell said. "Bone and witch! Let's just wash of the...!"

"What if it doesn't wash off?" Ned asked.

"So they are balls of paint that shoot from a gun? How do they go so far?" Webb asked.

"Bones and witches!" Wendell stormed off into our VFW.

Beans lowered the nozzle as if were dripping fire.

Some others were cussing now.

I looked around then looked across the street at a white blur that was a house.

"Four o'clock," Ned said. "Movement in that window."

I saw Beans tighten his grip on the nozzle.

Above was blue sky and a cool sun. The ghetto trees around our VFW were still barren, black and gnarly like the ones that steal and eat children. Cars whizzed by on 13 Mile Road and a rumbling semi made the water in our brown puddles vibrate. It was warmer but most everything around us was more dead than alive except the movement in the boxy house across the street.

"It's the TV house," I said.

Ned turned back. "Wash it off, Beans. Just wash it off," he said.

Beans let her rip, bracing as if the hose now had the kick of a 50 Cal.

The paint splats washed off.

Ned stooped and picked up a soluble shell bullet casing that once encased the paint. Clouds came and the wind picked up and we got cold just standing there watching the water. The air now had a damp chill.

Beans gave a cough, which reminded us all not to do too much on the first day above freezing. Beans and Webb walked inside and joined Wendell and looked over the sandwiches that Ned's wife had made.

Me and Ned lingered outdoors, looking at our white washed wall.

Ned stepped closer, held out a hand and traced a finger over a faded orange splat. He turned and I knew he could focus on the house. "I can still see you," he said. "You can't hide from me!" He turned and went inside.

I just looked at the paint marks. I could still see them. It takes more than water to wash some things away.

Pal stayed at the window. Red sat in front of his TV and Splinter looked at Cell.

"All I'm saying," Cell said, "Is that we shouldn't've ran straight into my house."

"I could've hit them," Pal said. "All I need is a couple of good balls and I can hit anything I see."

"Where else we gonna go?" Splinter asked. "And we're not running. We just walked in from the back door. We don't run from nothing!"

"Yea right. Like that's gonna fly with Deep Pockets! Who else has is gonna have paintball guns and break out windows! My neighbor? She's an old bag! All's I'm saying is we got to think it through. They'll call Deep Pockets back any second and then what are we going to do?" Cell asked. He was pacing now.

"We're not going to answer the door that's for certain! He don't have a warrant!" Splinter said.

"You think they can even see this far? They're lucky to find the door." Red said. "Trust me. My Granpa pees in the hallway if the light is off. Those geezers are the same way."

"And what was Pocket Rocket doing there?" Cell asked.

"They ratted us out because their broken window." Splinter said.

"I don't think so," Red said.

"Oh! So now you're an expert just cause you live with a grandpa?" Cell asked.

"Yes, I am. I know more about how old people smell and think than all of you put together. They have something that keeps them from ratting out stuff like this."

"What?"

"They don't want others to know they need help. Think about it. You think old people want strangers to wipe crap out of their own butts after they drop off the kids? Don't be stupid. They have their dignity."

"Calling the cops when you get shot at and calling a nurse when you're done letting the children out to play are two way different things!" Cell said.

Splinter nodded.

"Trust me," Red swore at them. "It's the same thing!"

Pal opened the curtain again. "If they don't like the cops any more than we do, that could make things really interesting."

7

ESCALATION

Us five old men stared at our new TV screen. It looked oddly out of place in a kitchen where the next newest appliance was a microwave from 1985.

"Right there's the enemy," Beans said.

"I don't see anything," Webb said.

Ned touched the screen, pointing a finger at a shadow. "Right there."

"How can an enemy be in Pocketville? Aren't you using the wrong word?" Wendell asked.

"Wendell's right," I said and left for the fridge at the far end of the room. "Have you forgotten what an enemy is?"

"There!" Beans pointed to the monitor. "He came after midnight. The limp tickler was thinking about it."

"About what?" I asked, returning.

"About being an enemy?" Wendell asked and smiled at me.

I shivered and looked at the drafty window. The pillow had come loose and I stepped to push it back and slipped. When I came to, I was on the table like Webb and the boys sat me up. I lurched a moment, thinking they were them. "What happened?" I asked.

"Slipped," Ned said.

"How?"

"Fixing the window," Ned pointed to the window.

"Shouldn't have to be up there to begin with." Webb said.

"Battles and witches!" Wendell said, storming back to the video monitor.

I got up, fixed the draft in the window and walked outside with Ned and Beans. We looked around.

The roads were quiet and no movement came from the houses across the street. A wind had come in from the west and it was below freezing again. A few lone snowflakes were lost in the air and having trouble finding the ground like the 82nd Airborne long ago.

Behind us, our VFW building settled in the breeze as decrepit as our bodies and looked like it just did a few bouts with a bayonet.

Well, we were just standing there waiting for the doves to poop on us, when I pointed. "Is that the house?" I asked Ned.

"Yup," Ned said.

"There and up there are the cameras," Beans said, pointing.

"I don't believe it." I pulled a pack of cigarettes. Beans and Ned each took one.

"What?" Ned asked. We went back inside.

"See that!" Wendell pointed to the screen where me, Beans and Ned had been captured and frozen on the video tape. "When did they start smoking?"

"I'll be." I said. "Looks like our normal speed."

"Battles and witches!" Wendell said.

"Then what?" I asked and looked at the four old men around me. "We're all worn out just by looking at the pictures."

They all looked at me and it was in their eyes. They knew I was right.

We went to the table and dealt cards.

Beans still had the biggest mouthful of Nazi teeth and last night he won my Lugar.

I was running out resources. I looked around.

All of us had out our little bits of treasure. They were laid on the table before us.

I looked away. It seemed all our bounties were getting smaller. Even for the ones with the biggest piles of stuff.

The next day the sun was out again. Two days in a row. Nearly a record. The land around the four corners became brown and bare

At dusk, two teenagers left the back door and circled around to the stand of pines.

"What do they do in there?" Cell asked, looking across 13 Mile Road from the shelter of trees with a pair of binoculars. "They don't even know we're here!"

Splinter started cussing. "Who cares what they do? I don't even believe I'm here! This is stupid!" He stood up and stretched and knocked the mud off his pants.

"Get down!" Cell grabbed Splinter but lifted himself to a standing position instead. He did feel a bit strange.

Its no fun spying on people who don't care they're being spied on. And they were teenagers after all.

Why were they spying in the first place? It was all starting to make them feel stupid.

Splinter turned to his friend, "All I'm saying is that this isn't real. It's not like the game!" Splinter then looked close at the V.F.W. and noticed something and crouched down, pulling Cell with him. "Gimme those!" Splinter took the binoculars. Through the lenses his eyes focused on a security camera mounted on the roof of the VFW. "You're not going to believe this!" Splinter said.

"What?"

Splinter handed Cell the binoculars. "Two o'clock. Security cameras on the roof."

"No way," Cell worked the focus.

"I think we got us a little war!" Splinter said.

8
BREAK-IN

I picked up some thick plexiglass at Pocketville Hardware and some silicone with the help of Brance, one of the grey-haired guys that shadowed me as soon as I entered the store.

"Sure you don't need help with that?" Brance asked again at the door.

"I'm good." I said.

"What's it for?"

"A window."

"A broken one?"

"Just one that's worn out."

"Did it break?"

"Just wore out. Like the rest of us," I lied and felt strange. Lying wasn't done in peace-time living.

"Need help installing it?" he asked and I looked at him.

"No. It's a confidence thing," I said and he took it well. He understood emasculation. Otherwise he wouldn't be working a job at his age for minimum wage in the first place. I felt sorry for him. Twenty years my younger and already missing the power of a job.

Back at the post, Ned and I set and glued her in and stood around panting.

"Let's the light in," Ned said.

"Ya," I said.

"What'd it cost?"

"Brance told Knoxal it was for The Post and they threw in the cost."

"Nice feller," Ned said. "They suspect anything?"

"No."

"Not even Brance?"

"No."

That night we had us a poker game in peace. We had a room with no moving shadows and no drafts. We got a chuckle out of Ned and his story about whacking some kid at Pocketville High with Bronx's arm. Good ole Bronx. They broke the mold after him. Yesterday he was one of us. Yesterday morning before we charged the Panzar Division.

Then the pelting came and we all looked at the window. A rainbow of splats pounded the new glass.

"Battles and witches!" Wendell said, his slippers whispered on the floor as he went for and opened the door. "Battles and witches!"

We didn't hear any car and see any dust and gravel. But we did hear kids laughing. Then all was quiet by the time we all made it to the door. "I don't like being laughed at." Beans said. "I hear them laughing."

"Let 'er be." Webb said. "Are they still there?"

"No." Ned said. "They're long gone."

"I still hear them laughing," Beans said.

We went back and dealt cards. I won back two teeth. I rolled them in my palm but only felt two things. They were cold and suddenly I didn't really care if I won the rest back or not. And worse yet, I felt that Beans didn't really care if he lost them. I looked over at Beans.

He was looking at paint on the outside of the window.

I looked at the paint too.

After the trucks left the VFW the four teenagers camped around Cells' TVs killed their game and went to the war window. Security cameras are kind of an invitation. A challenge. And for teenagers raised in a 9/11 world where weasel terrorists barely edged out space droids as real enemies, any threat was an opportunity to prove that they were special. That they were vital, contributing members of society.

So they left Cell's house and baseball-batted out the plexiglass. It had been cleaned from the paintball splats and it collapsed in relative ease. With an up-an-over, they slithered into the dark VFW hall, a dampy place that smelled like a bowling alley.

In the light of the open fridge, they finished off a few PBRs, took the smokes from a half empty carton and then started snooping around.

When they found the recorder, they just sat down, hit the rewind and started watching. The camera's had picked them up as they left the dark and stepped under the dome light.

"In we come!" Red said. "If she was digital, we'd be in focus."

Splinter tilted his head, as he watch himself smash out the window. Splinter rewound the tape. "Whoa!" Splinter said.

"Righteous. We've been filmed." Cell pushed the Eject button and pulled the tape and stuffed it in his coat. "We'll watch this at home. My mom's got one of these machines for her classics! Gotta pee?"

"Gotta pee!"

Cell wasn't stupid, he unplugged the VCR and turned it upright, jamming the door open with a pencil. The boys unzipped to spray the machine down.

"Marking territory!" Cell said and started laughing, and their streams crossed as they filled up the VCR.

Zipped and relieved, Splinter took up the cord. "Let's plug it back in!"

The four boys sat and watched the sparks snap in the machine and fog up burnt pee smoke until the circuit tripped and darkness fell.

They stumbled around until their eyes adjusted. Light from a car from 13 Mile moved across the room.

Pal saw something glow on a card table with chairs around it. He went to it and picked up two heavy little stones, just bigger than pebbles. He held them up to the moonlight to better see them glow and wondered why they held the light so well. He put them into his pocket to be examined later.

9

FLAGS AND FENCES

Frank's widow arrived to clean up the post for a mid-week wedding reception and noticed the break-in. She was a rounded, short lady, still carrying some plump into her old age. Her late husband proposed to her when she was thirteen. Frank was ten years her senior at the time and then the war started. On his return they had a passel of children, so she had seen her fair share of messes.

She phoned the Cap'n.

"You did the right thing by telling no one else. Keep it that way," Ned told her.

"Okay," she said. She was curious and all, but her late husband's military conditioning made her understand that one does not mess with the order of things.

Ned called his team in.

We arrived, left our diesels purring in the muddy lot and went inside.

"What?" Wendell asked.

"Stop complaining?" Ned said. "Ain't like you've anything else to do."

We circled the damage.

"This a first," Ned said.

"You're counting like the Brits," Beans said. "What about the windows, our trucks and them paintballing us? Ain't no first. Never was."

"What's Frank's widow gonna do?" Webb asked.

"Nothing," Ned said. "I told her to stay quiet."

"She's a woman," Webb said.

"I believe her. Frank was a good man," Ned said. "She'll walk in line."

"What are we gonna do?" I asked.

"Nothing," Wendell said.

I picked up the VCR by the cord. We all smelled enough burnt urine in our lives, a little more wasn't going to hurt. Piss dripped across the floor until I dropped it in the trash can.

"We can't do nothing now. We gotta mop up the place," Beans said.

"You really want to do nothing?" I looked in the eyes of the men around me.

They nodded and I shook my head.

It was as simple as that. By doing nothing we all knew it was going to happen.

One by one we turned away.

Thinking.

Imagining.

Remembering.

I turned away also.

Alone in our thoughts we were tallying up the cost of appeasement.

"No police," Beans said. "No need for them to get hurt."

"And it's our VFW," Ned said.

"Our 3946," Wendell said.

"Our Post," Webb said.

I looked around. They were waiting for me to say something but I didn't. And it didn't matter either way.

War was upon us.

Ignoring the drone of the TVs, four boys watched the pick-up trucks roll as they spied from Cell's basement window. They had all taken the day off because it was Wednesday and they had test.

They marked time by the groan of the floor above them as Cell's mom walked the triangle from the TV to the bathroom to the fridge and back to her couch every so often like a ship in the triangle trade.

"So. Doesn't matter," Cell said, spinning the low card across the table.

Red, Splinter and Pal went to the basement window to watch.

Cell climbed the steps, walked out his front door, crossed the street, entered VFW property and lowered the flag.

He swiped it in broad daylight then they rigged it on the makeshift pole in the back of Red's truck.

Red had a short flagpole in the bed of his truck where he flew the Rebel flag.

Red had red hair, red freckles and a red neck. He was Red. He had been shaving since Jr. High and had a thick goatee. He won a hundred dollar bet last year at his school for spitting over thirty feet. He drives his beat the death 4x4 truck with waist-high tires. Red drove around with the flag all that day.

Then they got back to their game. A team in Georgia was giving them some trouble. Johnny Rebs no doubt.

Red's truck was parked at Cell's house that night when a man with no right arm knocked on the door.

"Cell!" Cell's mom yelled.

"Get it yourself!" Cell yelled back up the steps.

The doorbell rang again and the floor creaked.

"Yes?" Cell's mom answered and looked at the empty right sleeve.

"Evening Ma'am." I pulled off a cap from my head.

"Yes?"

"My name's Lefty from across the street. Came to get our flag," I pointed to the old pick-up truck.

She leaned out her door and she saw it for the first time in the dim glow of the corner streetlight.

"Oh." Her voice faded of hope. "I'm so sorry," she turned and bellowed, "Cell!"

"No!" came a voice from deep down in the house. The mom tried to smile at me.

"He's a good boy." She said.

"I'll bet," I said and turned. By now Ned had used a small step ladder to get on the truckbed and was carefully detaching the flag, keeping it over his shoulder and out of harms way, he came back down. Flanked thirty feet off to the right was Beans. He was but a shadow. By the time Ned climbed down to the tailgate we noticed the four impotents watching us from a small basement window to the left of the front steps.

The big woman looked behind her and thought about inviting the man inside. "I'm so sorry," she spoke for herself. "Whatever they did I'm really sorry. Was that your flag?"

"Yours too, Ma'am," I said. "It's all of ours."

"Is it okay? We'll buy you a new one if you want. I think they have them at Dollar General™," she said.

"It's already been paid for, ma'am." I said and eased off the steps and joined Ned.

"We're so sorry," the mom said. She had that line down real good. Had lots of practice by the looks of things. Ned and I turned our back and left.

Beans stayed in the shadow for recon. He watched some cowards come up from the basement after the door shut. Through the picture window, he watched the fat woman slap her fat kid and saw the kid hit her back.

Battles and witches.

All day Saturday, those teenagers lounged on their porch and watched us put up our fence.

We didn't care. We were working. Sweat broke on our brows and we felt manhood.

Tools, equipment and friends busied themselves on our VFW property.

Wendell wiped his brow and looked across the street.

I walked up to him, so did Ned. "Battles and witches!" Wendell said, but his heart wasn't in it. The sun was out and warmth was in the air. A spring warmth. Fresh and alive it ate away our anger.

Fog from the river and some neighboring backyard ponds had burned off a few hours ago and a slight shadow was developing under trees because buds.

Beans joined us and we stared at the four boys.

They stared back.

Webb was off stretching the fence.

"Can you hit them from here?" Beans asked Ned.

Ned grunted.

Wendell and I smiled. You can see moon craters through Ned's sniper scopes.

"Battles and witches," Wendell said. "They didn't say sorry about the flag?" Wendell asked.

"The mom did," I said. Looking up, we saw our flag rippling in the spring air and light. We heard the halyards echo the aluminum pole. "Good to have it back," I said.

The day faded as the hands from the local hardware did the heavy lifting. The old east line wood fence now gave way to a spanking new chain-linker, complete with a sliding gate. It had a punch code as well as remote controls and moved on a track by a chain. New green mesh fencing now covered three of our four fronts. It continued along the south line and joined a new second gate, which we shared with an old white church.

As expected the fence raised the eyebrows of Knoxel and Branse from the hardware store.

Knoxel lost a boy to Vietnam and could look us in the eye.

We told him we were building a WWII weapons display for the town to visit next Memorial Day and wanted to make sure it was safe. But we found him snooping around.

Knoxal noticed the boys watching us too. "Riff raff little white negroes," he said, eyeing them.

But the fence had a calming effect. We all felt it around cards that night. The security cameras and been aligned better and the new VCR was locked up in a cabinet.

I was up another thirteen teeth.

Wendell and Beans still had dozens each, but no one had had a good hand for the last two hours.

I knew why.

All the men were thinking it.

But it was Beans who spilt the truth. "Fences never made any good neighbors in Europe," he said.

"True," I said, being up in the pot gave me the right to speak first.

"It looks better. Looks like the place is alive," Ned said.

"Locks better." Webb said. "I'm leaving my tractor tonight. Hope she does the trick."

We all looked at Webb and admired his hope. Of all of us he had the strongest faith. He still built things.

But a rage was circling around behind us and getting the flank. And there wasn't a one of us who could deny it. This was our piece of earth. Our Post. We dealt cards that night tired, but feeling good. The buzzing dome light at the door made us keep our eyes down and there was no wind.

That's why we didn't see it when we left.

10

NEW FLAGPOLE

Duke Dungy, a local boy with a college degree in journalism from Grand Rapids Community College had returned to Pocketville a few years ago. He was a tall, skinny young man who seemed to fit in because he asked intelligent questions and was soon given the town counsel beat.

He didn't dress up overly well and could hold his own with the farming end of Pocketville because he had a budget that allowed him to buy up any breakfast, lunch and dinner ticket he wanted. He truly loved a good cover story. Inspired by a John Grisham novel about small town papers making millionaires, he worked most of the hours in any given day in service to the Pocketville Triangle and its two thousand subscribers.

He owned the VFW story from its birth and ran the picture he had acquired on the front page the next day. He knew a good photograph could put Pocketville on the map and if it found its way into the the Associated Press or at least Fox News he could get the need leverage to go head to head with Woodward and Bernstein.

I heard about the attack from Brance at the hardware, where the story trumped the farmers talking about weather.

Ned got the news from Webb, who's wife was in a sewing circle with Frank's widow.

So by the time we called Beans the word was out and the damage done. But we called him nevertheless.

A slip-knot held the Abomination of Desecration to the top of our VFW flag pole, and all the retrieval lines were cut up high so the hideous thing couldn't come down. As it bannered, it brushed against our black P.O.W. Missing But Not Forgotten flag.

Far below, in the shadow cast by the Nazi flag, we were moving around like we had a plan. Webb had a chain out and was getting ready to secure it to the base of the flagpole and yank out the concrete foundation.

Ned was pushing a few bystanders who had come from Pocketville Hardware with Brance. He had a .45 behind his belt and was going to shoot off the brass clamps that held flag to the rope.

Each old farmer held a spanking new shovel. Compliments to Knoxel the manager at Pocketville Hardware no doubt. They were going to dig out the concrete and lower the pole nice and easy.

But it was Beans who took the alpha role when he pulled into our parking lot. He saw it and never put on the brakes.

People jumped out of the way.

Beans stomped his gas pedal and his truck toppled the whole darn flagpole, slamming Hitler's symbol of the Master Race into the mud and running it over before circling around and bringing his truck to the stop.

I smiled. Good ole Beans. That man could do a job!

An old farmer and Brance nearly got themselves beheaded because the pole came down without a timber right between them. They now know Beans and danger are one.

But in the end, it didn't really matter because Duke Dungy, Pocketville Triangle Executive Reporter who wanted to double his subscribers, ran the photograph front page the next day. He ran it in full color.

He also had the photo of the flag being crushed under Bean's bumper. That man knew how to take an action shot. He told us he planned to use that one in the next issue. He was thinking three days ahead for that photograph.

Today's article wasn't a big one. Didn't need to be. Any picture that showcased a Nazi flag bantering in the wind above an upside-down Stars and Strips and our black P.O.W. flag said enough. Said a thousand words too many if you asked me.

Our V.F.W. Post 3946 was in the background. The newspaper title and paragraph read: "Shameful Coward Shame"—Disgraced the Pocketville VFW Post 3946 last Sunday morning. The 'act of cowardly defiance', according to Police Chief Tabbs, 'marks a new era of darkness for area anarchists,' but city officials are proud to stand by their Veterans and raise new flag and pole donated by Pocketville Hardware. . ."

Duke Dungy's story went on to speak of the Joint Ceremony with Pocketville Fire and Police Departments, and how they aided their Veterans in restoring dignity to the Post and how fantastic community spirit of Pocketville outshines the morons who wanted to ring their little bells.

Dungy himself was there later that day and took more photographs which he ran in the very next issue. It showed us WWII guys re-raising the flagpole.

It showcased Beans, Webb, Wendell and Ned doing some replanting. It ran in the next issue on the front page with more pizzazz than Hitler's crisscross. It was the Marines from the South Pacific conquering Iwo Jima all over again.

I was just off the picture holding a shovel as if I knew what end to use. I joined some and gave the ground a few wacks, then Duke Dungy left and took the farmers with him. It was getting on towards dinner and he was Jesus feeding the masses again.

We declined the invitation.

They all left and we were alone.

We closed the gate to keep curious people away. We were spread out around the new cement under our flags. It was just us old ones. We weren't teary eyed. We were just quiet.

Until Webb spoke.

"She really said that?" Webb asked. "I don't like it."

"What are we gonna do?" I said.

"Battles and witches!" Wendell said.

"That fat woman doesn't know what to do and wants us to do something. She's pathetic. Wants us to do the parenting she never could," Webb said. "Said if we didn't talk to them she was gonna rat them out to the cops. Even though one of them is her kid."

"Let 'er do it!" Ned said. "It's easiest."

"That's her words?" Beans said.

"Ya. I heard her crying her story to Webb," Wendell said. "Sad lady."

"Desperate because those idiot kids," Webb said.

"Battles and witches come from pathetic bitches." Wendell said.

"They know what their doing. Hilter's children did too." I said. "Ain't her fault. It's their fault. But if they are working this hard find a fight, it can't be good. What are you men thinking?" I didn't have to ask the question. I already knew the answer.

Army men only think one way.

"Got me an idea." Beans said. And he told us.

We just looked at each other and then at the house across the street. Then we went inside our post.

Under the dark paneling, décored in bayonets, bands of dummy ammunition and other military paraphernalia, we dealt cards.

Beans wasn't bluffing when he pulled out the Lugar and put in on the table. He had a straight.

After we folded, Webb handed him the Nazi flag, and Beans laid the flag on the table and sat an old box next to it. From his box he took the German Lugar, 9mm pistol and worked the action, then handed another Lugar to Wendell who did the same.

"Seems fine," Wendell said, "but they always do before they jam."

"That's why we got two," Beans unzipped a plastic baggy filled with ancient ammo and we watched him and Webb stuff two clips full and racked shells into the chamber.

Wendell flipped on the safety and stuffed it deep into his pocket.

Beans wasn't the type who believed in safety's. He put the live weapon under the flag next to a video game Wendell had taken from his grandkids.

"That original ammo?" I asked.

Beans smiled.

"Sure it'll fire?" Wendell asked.

"It's German, ain't it?" Webb said. "It'll fire. They know how to do war."

Then Beans shredded the flag, passing his knife blade through the fabric as if it was cutting through a thick fog. He used the ribbons to cover the gift and his weapon and then left the building.

It was nearing dusk.

All we could do was effort our way to the window and watch. Webb was gonna go, but then decided not to. We knew why. Webb had a nice streak.

Beans just walked across road and knocked on the door with the butt of his hand. Wendell stood off some distance and leaned against a tree and lit up a smoke.

"He's at the door," Ned said, his right eye peering though the scope on one of his M1 rifles. His right index finger was extended along the chamber above the trigger. "A bunch of them are in front of him."

"Think Beans will be okay?" Webb asked.

Ned never responded.

None of us had too. None of us were worried about Beans.

11

SINGLE-HANDED FORAY

The tallest boy seemed to have the most hot air. But the fat one was in front. Beans recognized Red from Lefty's description, but kept a weather eye on the one in the back. Beans didn't trust that one.

That one had long straight black hair that covered his eyes. The hair swung off to one side as he looked around, but then the kid's head shifted and his eyes hid behind their cover again.

Beans gave that one, blackie hair, most of his attention despite never looking towards him.

"What?" shaggy blond asked.

"I got something in your flag for you." Beans said.

"What? Another arm! You can keep it!" Plump Tummy said. He had remembered Cap'n from school.

Beans nearly smiled at hearing this, but his mouth didn't work that way. "It's a video game," Beans said.

"Oh," the fat one said and looked at the others.

"We probably already got it," the red one said and held out his hand.

The fat one stepped up. He wanted the gift.

"Is this your house?" Beans asked the plumpy. The chunk nodded, keeping his hand out, fat fingers open.

"Then invite me in."

The fat kid looked at his friends, then stepped back.

"What's your name?" Beans asked.

"Cell."

"Your cave down there, Cell?" Beans motioned to the steps to the cellar. "After you."

Cell led. The others parted to let Beans pass.

He was a small, old man. Thin to the bone caring a ripped Nazi flag. His left hand took the rail. Down into a dungeon of a room that reeked of asthma Beans went. He didn't care. He had gone into dark places before. Bat caves were nothing new to him. Japs had gnawed out the hills of half the Pacific Islands. Hundreds of feet deep in some places. He lost count of how deep he had gone.

"We ain't like most," the fat kid said after they all reached the basement floor. "You mess with us and you get the best."

"Sounds tasty," Beans said.

"What did you do to our flag, old man?" the red goatee asked.

Beans handed him the Nazi flag. Shredded, the flag fell off in strips, exposing the game and allowing Beans 9mm 1938 German Lugar to come into play.

Focused on the flag, Red never looked at his comrades. "You wasted my flag," Red said, then he went still and quiet.

The others were still. Very still.

Beans palmed his 9mm Lugar. It was pointed at the belly of the red kid. But Beans was a fair man, as he spoke each boy got a turn to feel the open end of the muzzle aimed at their innards.

"My name is Captain Allen Mitchel, K Company," Beans moved the open barrel along. Beans knew it was a first for them. He melted then.

"This is a German Lugar taken from a decayed Nazi in pillbox at Normandy. I wasn't in Normandy. I won it in a poker game the other night." Beans pointed it at the TV and depressed the trigger, exploding the screen, sending glass and smoke through the room.

None of them could hear anything but ringing of thunder.

"It's only for close combat," Beans said after the stun moment passed. You boys get against that wall."

They did.

Stereo and electronic toys started exploding as Beans worked the trigger, bullets shattering stuff. Smoke stung their young eyes.

Then he leveled the gun at the boys again.

Cringing from the impact concussion, their hands were over there ears. Each saw the weapon pointed at them once again. One dribbled his pants. But one of them was just still. The dark haired one. Blackie, The one with hidden eyes.

Beans held the gun on that boy. His finger went white on the trigger as blood flowed away from pressure.

The black-haired teenager wanted to push his hair away from his eyes, but he dared not move. He didn't want to send a challenging signal to that old man. He knew the veteran wanted him to move. The soldier was begging him to flinch. To twitch. To breath. To die.

Then the plump one took a step forward. "Come on, tough guy!" Cell made a fist and pounded it against his chest like an ape. "Put a round were it does some business!"

Beans turned the weapon and fired two shots into the boys chest so close together they sounded like one. They both struck the fat kid in the diaphragm. A quarter could have covered both holes.

Cell went down. Hard. Opening some of his scalp on the cement, he went fetal and withered.

Beans put the barrel back on Blackie. He held back his surprise, not seeing the fat kid as the type to die for a belief. Oh well, he'd been wrong before. And he killed the wrong men before.

"Looks like we drew first blood." Beans said. "No surprise there. Stop funning with Post 3946 or we'll kill rest of you. We stopped scum before. We stopped nations of scum. Scum Empires. We can stop you three!"

A small electrical fire had started in the TV and sparks now climbed some wire and more flame broke. But the barrel never moved off the Blackie as the one on floor withered, dying.

Beans eyed a fifth of whisky that had fallen to the floor from a desk. "Pass me that, Blackie."

Pal did, stepping over Cell's body.

Bean's spun off the top with one flick of his left thumb, took a swig and wiped his mouth with his sleeve. The Lugar never moved. "Since he'll soon be dead and we might have war after all, here's the rule. The team who calls the cops loses!" Beans backed to the steps, listening to electric sparks flicker in the dungeon. Smoke was starting to billow up the stairs. An alarm started beeping. Beeping loud.

"But you three don't want war. War is us at our worst." He nodded to the VFW. "And it's us at our best. As to your thoughtless injustice?" Beans tossed the bottle of whiskey to the floor near the body of the youngster he double lunged then put a round into the bottle, spraying alcohol into the flame, igniting most of the room and the carcass of the shot boy on fire. "I don't like it! You leave us be! You go fight someone else."

Wendell came back from the window. "The smoke has stopped. Looks like your fire is out."

Beans grunted.

"Battles and witches!" Wendell said. "You lit the place on fire?"

"Now they'll change their shorts and re-think the whole thing." Ned said, eyeing his cards

"One might not be able to think," Beans said. "I'll take two," he discarded two.

"You bully young 'uns a little too big to cry to momma and you think they think?" I asked.

"They've been told they're special by their liberals since birth. And now they're figuring it ain't true?" Webb said. "Every generation has a learning curve."

Beans listened for sirens. He knew it was his last hand with his friends for a long time. You don't murder an unarmed boy without trouble. He was trying to figure out what happened to him. Then he gave up figuring. He had bigger things to figure than that if he opened the figure jug. His ears were still good. The sirens would come soon.

I got up and pulled a PBR from the fridge and walked to the front door and looked out. Our new gates were closed tight. I closed and locked the door again. I took a swallow of cold beer and turned back down the hallway. Going by the fridge, I took up the rest of the sixpack for the men.

I had to admit it.

I felt more alive than I did yesterday.

12

Aftermath

Splinter, Cell, Red and Pal didn't talk much after the shooting. When they did they had nothing to say. Their stuff had just been shot to Shatterville.

"What's your mom gonna say?" Splinter asked, holding ribbons of the fascist flag and looking at Cell.

"Nut 'un," Cell said from a white face. Red and Pal went to him and got his clothes off. They were now smoldering in whiskey smoke on the floor.

"She'll go to the cops," Pal said.

"Can you stand?" Red asked.

"No," Cell said.

"She's gonna come down here. You really don't think she'll come down here?" Splinter asked.

Cell looked around. "No. And can you shut up for a second?"

"You see how he looked at us? I thought he was gonna do us all!" Red said. "And how'd he know you were wearing your Kevlar?"

Pal ran his finger inside Cell's bullet proof vest. It was still on the boy's body because Cell was hurt too much to take it off.

There was no penetration. One bullet went for soft stomach, the other nicked the edge of a rib.

Cell flinched hard as Pal pulled his hand back and held it up to the light looking for blood.

"No blood," Pal said.

Cell turned left and puked hard. Another level pain then ignited from a chipped rib and forced another convulsion. His guts were reacting to something. "You sure

I ain't bleeding?" Cell whispered and rolled on the floor half fetal, his hair falling in his own mustard.

"You ain't bleeding none," Pal said and looked at Red. "That old man never knew he was wearing Kevlar. How could he?"

"No way." Splinter said. He had a wet spot in his jeans and kept his coat hanging below his crotch. He didn't convince anyone.

They all saw it in the old man's eyes. Indifference. The man didn't care a flying feather who he dropped the bomb on. It was the first time any of them had seen a killer face to face.

Pal looked around and poked at stuff. Life wasn't being fair to him. No one seemed to notice that he had barrel at his belly more than the others until Cell piped his Pepto.

A spark snapped. "Whoa! Cell you gotta unplug all you stuff," Splinter said.

Cell moaned. "Do it," he said, cheek to the cement in unburnt whiskey.

"Hang on, Cell," Pal said. "I'm just gonna lift you out of your puke."

"He really tried to kill me," Cell said.

TV glass popped under their shoes and some loose stuff fell from shelves as the area settled.

"It's still happening." Red said. "We gotta unplug everything."

"Whoa!" Splinter said. "You can still smell the gunpowder." Then he turned around. "It's all trashed!" He picked up an Armegeddon DVD from the floor. "Good movie!" He lobbed it to Pal.

"That'll still work?" Pal nodded to the computer in the corner.

"Yea. Cap'n must have not seen it," Cell said, his white face going green.

"What are we gonna do?" Red asked.

"I can't think down here," Splinter said.

Cell started shaking a little.

"No cops, huh? Now that's got potential," Pal said.

"Why'd he try to kill Cell? All we were doing is messing with their old building," Spinter said. "And their flag."

They all looked at each other. Splinter and Red shook their heads.

"My Grandpa would," Red said. "He's ornary."

"Whatta ya mean?" Cell asked.

"I don't think he was bored. Do you? He wasn't over there playing with his TV remote." Red said. "He's not a nursing home man. He wasn't the typed to retire in St. Petersburg."

Cell had a hand under his vest along his guts. Something wasn't working inside him. He was swelling. He felt blood pulsing to the area.

Pal turned the DVD of Armageddon in his hands.

"What do you got in mind?" Red asked.

Pal looked at the DVD and cleared the computer station and brought the tool online. "I like the scene where the NASA Commander Dude tells Bruce Willis that he wouldn't trust his crew with potato guns." In a few minutes of fingering on Google, Cell brought up a webpage.

The room started to smell more like an electrical fire than a fire fight.

Splinter picked up seven shell casings.

Then the two of them came in and stood behind Pal.

Cell tried to stand and did so. He looked at the screen and took hold of Splinter's shoulder to still the spinning room."What are we now? Plumbers?" Cell asked.

"Those are the best!" Red said.

"No way!" Splinter was hooked. He knew art when he saw it.

"Let's downgrade the weapons," Pal said. "Let's just drive them crazy and do it from a safe distance. We'll never get trapped inside again."

"What is it?" Cell asked.

"It's a potato gun, moran!" Pal said and printed off details.

Ned leaned forward and for a moment I thought he was trying to see my cards. Then he stood up and went to the video surveillance.

Webb saw the truck go by on the TV screen. "Where they off to now?" he asked.

"Don't really care," Ned said, "But I don't really like it when they are all moving about in the same direction."

"All?" Beans asked.

"Yea."

"All four?"

"Yes."

"Impossible," Beans said.

"Why's that?" I looked at Beans.

Beans now stood and went to Ned and they looked at the empty road on the TV.

"Can you play it back?" Beans asked.

Ned unlocked the cabinet and rewound the recorder.

We all watched four boys leave their house and get in a truck and wheel on by. A fat boy needed help getting up into the lifted truck.

"It can't be!" The etched groves in Beans face hardened. Drained of passion, he went to the table and sat down. Sat hard.

I reached out to stable him but he brushed me off.

Webb looked at me.

Ned came and sat and looked at us.

Wendell gathered the cards, shuffled and dealt. "What's the big deal?"

Beans stared at Wendell, forcing the man's eyes to drop. Then he took up his cards and had a look. His hand went to the pile of gold teeth in front of him and scooped them. They were cold. To think he had almost bet the stack on two pair. He grunted, smiled and stopped listening for cop sirens.

13

COUNTER-ATTACK

Deep in the stand of pines, four boys huddled around a pile of potatoes as the last of the grey drained from the sky. There were now circles of light under the lamps at the four four way stop and the V.F.W. parking lot.

"How far they shoot?" Splinter asked, squinting to see the enemy camp beyond the branches.

"Six, maybe eight hundred feet. Maybe a bit more," Pal said. "But potatoes are heavy. It's a mass against a constant sort of thing."

"What are you talking about?" Red asked.

Pal pointed at the VFW.

"From here?" Cell asked, sweat beading above is lip despite the cold. His left hand stayed on his stomach where the skin twitched above some welts they grew yesterday. Steam swirled from his wet hair. His body was running a little warm from working overtime. "No way!" He sat on a log.

Red looked at Pal. So did Splinter.

Pal reached in the pile and pulled out a potato. "What? You going to wait around until they shoot us down?"

Beyond the fence rested a row of five trucks and beyond that sat the enemy encampment. It was now dark. Two days had passed.

"How long you think they'll be in there?" Cell asked. He looked behind him whenever possible. Any sign of trouble and he was going to drift into the darkness. Running was beyond him, but he could hide. He new some good spots that wouldn't upset his rib.

"Dunno." Splinter said. "But they can't stay in there forever."

Pal looked around. He then showed them how to spray the barrels and ram a potato load. Uncapping the larger compression chamber at the base of the PVC gun, he sprayed the aerosol into the pipe and screwed the end down. All the boys did the same.

Pal then shouldered his potato launcher as if it were a standard marine issued Stinger Missile. He depressed the red button of the ignition spark and the sharp recourse of chemical explosion compressed the air canister and exploded the potato out the barrel. The boys watched dumbfounded as the spud sailed over the ground they had just walked and slammed into Cell's house.

"Why my house?" Cell asked.

"Practice," Pal said. Red and Splinter fired and missed. Cell shot and scored. He spud disintegrating on impact.

"Ouch," Cell said, holding himself, his face turning a shade of purple.

After another round of practice, the boys were ready to engage the enemy and were quickly reloading. Content that they could hit the broad side of a Cell's house, they hunkered down.

"What's the distance?" Splinter asked. "It looks farther away."

"About six hundred feet," Cell said as if reading a range finder.

"Are we ready for this?" Red asked.

"Why?" Splinter asked.

"Cause it's an offensive," Red said. "We will offend them."

"He offended me and my room," Cell said. "I'll show them offensive. And I'd like to know how he knew I had a vest." Cell moved his barrel towards the feet to prepare the weapon.

Pal and Red looked at each other, then they loaded and raised their barrels and tapped them for luck as if giving toast. They brought them up to their shoulders and for the next ten minutes, fired at will, smashing dozens of potato into the building. They busted out windows, knocked loose siding and jarred the door off its hinges. The fence wasn't high enough to shred their spuds and truck windows blew out, busting the safety glass into a tiny pieces.

But most of their spud power went to the VFW itself. It was larger and they each thudded it with four straight volleys.

"How come no one's coming out?" Cell wanted to know. They others bumped their shoulders, not able to answer.

They didn't know soldiers took cover during barrages.

Wendell picked up the remains of a potato that had rocketed across the room and returned to the video monitor. "Battles and witches! Happy now, Beans? Idaho just declared war on us!"

"Look at that!" Ned said. "They're in the trees."

"Bunched together. No flank," Webb said.

"Looks like they got your window, Webb." I said.

"Battles and witches!" Wendell said.

"What are you thinking, Beans" Webb said. "You proud of yourself for prodding those youngsters?"

"Ask Ned," Beans said.

No one did. We just hunkered down behind the TV and watched the assault. After one particular loud crack of a spud hitting the wall, we looked at each other.

"What did you say to those kids at Pocketville High this year?" I asked Ned.

He smiled.

"I don't believe it!" Webb said. "I see it in your eyes! You two like this!"

"What about you?" Beans asked.

"Me? No way. Count me out. But at least I'm acting like I know how a war ends," Webb said.

"How's that?" Ned asked.

"Everybody loses," Wendell said.

I looked around, checking the control area for intruders. Webb could yap all he wanted. I knew how I felt. As a kid, war made me grow up. Made us all grow up. So we did and quick. It aged us forty years in as many minutes. I remember going from eighteen to fifty-eight the first time a bomb exploded one of my buddies to pieces. Many a soldier was lost by being impaled by the bones of his buddies. I looked around at my fellow veterans.

This little feud seemed to be aging us back to 58 again. Maybe war was the fountain of youth.

"We're sitting ducks if they get inside," I said.

We were all thinking it, but I was the one who said it. It woke us up to the fact that we were unprepared.

"There are things worse than losing, Ned. Things worse than losing. Let's ask for help," Webb said.

"You want to ask a ticket totter to tackle the toddlers?" Beans asked. "I don't believe it?"

"Ahh. You're right," Webb said. "We can handle this."

Beans nodded and started giving orders. He sent me to check the north flank. Webb took the west. Ned the East. Wendell held the front and after a while, the potatoes stop falling and Ned saw the boys rise and leave and drive off in a truck with a Rebel Flag flapping in the air. A few toots of a horn taunted us as it drove off.

"Battles and witches!" Wendell said.

Beans called us in and started talking and what he said would have been funny if it wasn't so scary.

We went back to the table and sat.

"Good thing we had the fence up." Webb said. "It could have been a lot worse."

We dealt a few more rounds but the betting was off, we just played out the hands that were given as our conversations reached out and started doing inventory on our resources.

Our hobbies that we each have been nesting on for decades were no longer pastimes. They were getting leveraged into our war.

The first thing we agreed upon was acquiring the psychological advantage.

That was a gimme.

14

Casualty

Frank's widow and Webb's wife met for lunch once a week. Neither drove much anymore, but by hook or snook they somehow they always managed to get together for a light sandwich at the Deli by the Pocketville Dam. Both women were frail. Webb's wife was thin as a wippit. Frank's Widow was a dumbling. Their eyes were getting covered by their upper eyebrows.

"What's going on?" Webb's wife asked.

"What?" the widow replied.

"Webb's busy. Too busy even for that beaver."

"What's he been doing?" Frank's Widow asked. She took bit from her chicken wrap, bobbing her head to the shaking of her hands and then stared out the window until she chewed it. "I miss the birds," she said.

"You know my Webb, his life is his pole barn. He's got the men out there now," she laughed. "Smoke was rolling out the door like they were burning trees. Good for them."

"Why don't you just ask him? He's your husband," the dumpling said.

"You know those men. It would be easier to dig up your Frank and get the answer out of him than get those men to square with you."

At this the widow smiled.

One thing women of WWII soldiers all have in common is a bizarre smorgasbord of dysfunctional communication. They were quiet for a few minutes to respect the awkwardness of each others lives.

Then they got to talking about important things like obituaries and the ailments of normal folk at the Four Corner Church.

World War Two produced 48,347 M4 Sherman Tanks. So it's only natural for a few to be laying around here and there for the picking up. And since Webb had owned a small trucking company from '58 to '65, he had snagged a few from the crusher under general stewardship principles.

Five to be exact.

His wife didn't care. It got him out of the house and kept him rodent teething on hobbies that she deemed a whole lot more constructive than some of his Pabst drinking cronies.

At first she got nervous when she saw them in different positions in his big pole barn when she brought out sandwiches. The Sherman tanks worked. He let his grandchildren drive them around on the farm once in a while when they came up to visit from Texas.

Right now Webb and the brothers got four them running and opened the barn doors to ventilate exhaust. One burned a little rich. Then they checked the turrets and some other basic systems.

One Sherman tank was a parts tank and had been gutted. Hooking a chain to it, they broke free the rust on the tracks and got her rolling. Externals looked terrific. Webb had them all looking identical in flat military green with a trim white star on their sides.

On the parts tank, the 74mm cannon was frozen in place with six decades of rust and the wheels groaned fingernail on chalkboard as they turned. Most important was the hatch. It had a good strong hatch.

Webb knew that hatch well and took out his welder with the boys and made some minor modifications to it.

"It won't work," Wendell said. "No one's that stupid."

"There's four," Webb said. "The odds say it will."

Beans grunted and looked hard at Webb when he said the number four.

"Maybe it will," I said. Mobs aren't the smartest. I mean, look what happened when we derailed the German trains. Krouts almost killed each other when we knocked 'em off schedule."

Ned looked at Beans.

Those two knew something.

"It'll work. Every kid in the world wants to see in a tank," Webb said.

We all looked at each other. The others left for dinner. I ate with Webb and his Mrs. We speculated when the robins would be flying back home.

Then the two of us went back to his barn.

"Just follow behind in your truck," he said. "She'll just roll along now that she's leashed." The chains were short, making certain the second tank would track behind the first. Seeing those 74's coming out from their turrets brought back some memory. The lead one was running. Rumble and roar took me back aways.

I was glad it was dark because my face was coming alive with emotion. My eyes sweated. I waved to Webb's Mrs. upon leaving and followed him onto the road.

She looked sad and didn't wave back. At least I think she looked sad. She was a bit blurry standing their alone under her front porch light.

Ten minutes later we approached and V.F.W. and Webb was a happy man. He grinded his M4's over the asphalt leaving some grooves when the treads plowed under as he turned. The gate opened before us as we rumbled into the yard. They seemed to slide more out of fear than obedience and Beans, Ned and Wendell stepped out of the shadows to meet us.

Since one Sherman was dead on its tread, it took some finagling to get it pointed just right.

We didn't just push it around.

It takes a tank to move a tank.

When done, the 74mm cannon aimed straight into that fat kid's TV house.

Webb pulled the pins, dropped the chains and then parked the other Sherman on the other side of the flagpole, aiming it at the same house and shut down the motor after idling it a bit to let her cool.

All five of us were there in and around the circle of light from our dome light. We took up bags of mulch and dumped it around the tracks, landscaping those tanks all nice and pretty.

Webb locked down his functional M4 and we left the gutted Sherman's hatch open.

"Nice," Beans said. "Very nice."

"Really think it'll work?" Wendell asked.

Webb nodded.

None of us saw the potato hit Wendell, shattering his glasses and tearing out a wall of fake teeth. Another potato round splattered off the M4 without making so much as a thump. Those things had some thick hide.

But I heard Wendell's teeth clinking across the armor. Blood gushed. Then more rounds of spuds started impacting the building and parking lot. We were low enough that the fence shredded the next rounds. Beans was under Wendell now with his back to the tracks. Bean's shirt front was covered in blood of a buddy once again. Ned and Webb were gone.

I stood and stormed across the lot in a hard walk, incoming whistling around me like the old days. If one brought me down, another man would take my place.

They couldn't get us all.

I reached my truck and brought it around, sheltering Wendell and Beans from the incoming. We had Wendell loaded and with just a little huff and puff and we were all inside my truck, down below the metal, wary of the glass.

I saw them run to the fence. One poked his pipe through the crack and my window went white with mush and I stomped the gas.

Whether the ambush stopped or was just starting we didn't care. That last potato blurred my window good, filling it with cracks. Another took out a headlight before we rounded the corner for the expressway.

Ned rode shotgun and I used his eyes.

"I saw four of them, Wendell," Ned said. "One hitting you like that was just luck."

We liked how Ned spoke and it calmed Wendell, whose head was now bleeding on Bean's arm and Webb was nearly on the floor so Wendell could stretch out.

Ned kept talking to Wendell. Keeping him calm and counting down the minutes as we evaced him.

Wendell was alert and listening. I saw Bean's eyes in the rearview mirror.

Wendell heard one thing from Ned. Webb, Beans and I heard another.

Though Ned was saying all the reasons he'd be fine, we knew it was out of our hands.

By the time the boys stopped running, they all had good branch rash across their faces. They were alone in a the low river forest and the rustling of high branches hinted that a breeze was about. Far away the drone of a river factory could be heard. Not that they were listening. They laughed, puffed and coughed.

Cell had fallen far behind and could be heard cursing the darkness and the cold. Minutes later, He made it to them. His lips were blue and he staggered in holding his stomach and chest with both hands. He puked again after he stopped and looked for blood in the vomitous.

"What's wrong with you?" Splinter asked.

"Dunno. Just hurts." He swore.

"Where?"

"Where? Where I got shot, stupid!"

They then crossed the Rails to Trails State Park project that converted a derelict railway track to a bike path and were near the parking area and Red's truck.

Red didn't want to park near the VFW. He liked his truck.

"That was awesome!" Splinter repeated. "We got them at the tanks!"

Pal was looking around. "We got trouble." Pal said. "Big trouble."

They looked at him.

Pal had been shooting potato guns for two years and knew what a good round spud could do. He didn't even want a body shot, just a duster that would drop the old men in their mud for what they done to Cell's room. Pal didn't care about the others and their marksmanship. You just don't pick up a potato gun and hit what you shoot at in the dead of night. He knew they'd be lucky to splat one against the building in the dark.

But Pal saw his round drop a man. An old man. And he knew by the behavior of the vets that someone had fallen hard.

No yelling or scolding came there way.

An old man. A friend, a lifelong friend had gone down. A WWII soldier had just been sniped by a spud from Pal's potato gun.

"I say we go to the cops and lose," Pal said.

"What?" Splinter challenged.

"Why?" Cell asked.

"I dropped one. Head shot." Pal said.

"That serious?" Red was by the truck.

"Yea."

"How serious?" Splinter asked.

"You want me to shoot you in the head?"

No one answered.

"Wouldn't it just bounce off?" Splinter asked in a low tone.

"I don't think I hit him in the back of the skull," Pal said. "Maybe I did. Or it could have been one of you guys. But I think we busted a face. I know I busted a face."

They looked at each other. Then they walked into the open and loaded the guns in the back of Red's truck and drove away.

"Well it serves them right for busting up my stuff and shooting me," Cell said. "I ain't right."

"What ain't right?" Splinter asked.

"My guts ain't right. Ain't right at all."

"You got a busted rib," Red said. "It ain't supposed to be right."

Cell nodded. But deep inside, his innards seemed to be retracting in a way that made him not care about his broken rib.

We didn't need no doctor to tell us that Wendell needed more than a dentist. I slowed down after a while, knowing I was driving angry.

Wendell sat up and spit out the last of a broken tooth. "Thons of itches!" Wendell said.

Ned and the others were looking out the windows. We all were thinking the same thing. We had gotten ambushed by some kids. We had forgotten how quick stuff could happen.

"You think you'll get another Medal of Honor for this?" Webb asked. Wendell smiled and winced. A dirty, leather, snow-shoveling glove had been jammed into his mouth to stem the bleeding and it was now soaked in neon red blood.

"It's never too late to earn another medal." Beans said. "But you don't need to prove anything to anyone anymore. You've done enough."

"attles and itches!" Wendell uttered. It takes more than a rag to stop some from cussing.

"We will prove them!" Webb said.

"We should be straight on the story," Ned said.

"I 'ust fell! Wendell uttered, more blood came out his nose as he did so.

I accelerated my Crew Cab F340 to 95 miles an hour. A record. Ned helped and told me when to slow. We were nearing the big city.

Ned looked at me when Beans spoke of Wendell's Medal of Honor.

Beans had one too, but he never respected Wendell's until now. Had always cheapened Wendell's because Krouts weren't cruel in the Asian sense of the word. Nazi's were killers and efficient ones at that, building their death factories and all. But they were still human compared to what Beans had seen.

So Beans had always talked of Wendell's medal as plastic, compared to the ones fished out in the Pacific. The fact that Bean's now respected Wendell meant something.

Ned pointed down the highway for me to keep speeding. He thought so too.

"All abuse victims say they fell," Webb said.

"Are we going to call the cops?" I asked.

Wendell shook his head. Hard.

Webb shook his head too. The others agreed. We stared into the night. Five men in a truck going to the hospital. Going fast. The lines and headlights blurred and if was bumpier, slower and colder it could have been another time and place.

"It's going to get worse before it gets better," I said.

No one replied. I knew they disagreed with me. I knew I was wrong after I spilt the words.

War never, ever gets better.

"Who owns those trees?" Beans asked. "We can't even hate Elvis pinned down by those trees."

"The Mart family," Ned said.

"We're sitting ducks with those trees out there," Bean's said.

"I know Marty Mart," Webb said. "I'll take care of those trees."

"It's next exit," Ned said. "Slow down."

I did. I had a cracked windshield and a busted headlight and couldn't see that great to begin with. "I'm reporting that I hit a deer. That ain't going to the cops, is it?"

"No," Beans said.

"That's insurance fraud," Webb said.

"So," I said. "If I'm gonna be a liar again, I might as well get paid for it."

15

Tank Trap

The tree limbs hanging above the road blurred over the windshield as the four boys cruised in Red's truck. They passed houses set deep off the roadway with long winding driveways as they circled back around towards Pocketville.

Soon they came back to the boring, straight roads, built from trails with homes that got splattered by snow when they Counties plowed the avenues. Mailboxes, each bent to the will of curling snow, passed by Cell's window and stirred his stomach to growl. But he was still to afraid to eat.

"We gotta get off the road. Or at least dump the guns," Pal said.

"Let's cruise by the VFW." Splinter said.

"Too dangerous," Red said.

"Then how am I going to get home?" Cell asked.

"Whatever," Red said and turned back towards the VFW.

All was quiet in the truck. Not even the tunes were playing. They drove closer.

"Don't stop," Pal said. "Just drive on by."

Red braked at the four-way stop and paused.

They looked.

Across the way was the VFW. Its farmlight lit up the door. The tanks were nestled in shadow and gloom because they didn't reflect color or light. They looked like they didn't belong there.

Above the green monsters, the spotlighted flag caught the breeze and showed its color. All else beyond the compound was dark.

The boys looked at each other.

"Shouldn't those tanks be like be overseas or somewhere?" Cell asked.

"Like inside you mom's TV?" Splinter said.

"Some soldiers," Red said. "They left their gate open."

"Too bad about the cameras. I'd like to get a better look at the tanks," Pal said. "We should stop and pick up the potatoes if we do anything. Start destroying evidence."

"You think you can get on the roof and smash their two cameras, Splinter?" Red asked. "You get the cameras, I'll get the tape."

"Deal," Splinter said.

"We gotta get the tape if we're gonna know how bad Pal nailed his geezer. Wouldn't mind watching that a time or two!" Red said.

Cell nodded to him. "That's right! It ain't real until we make it on TV."

Red turned north from the four-way and they accelerated past the VFW on their left.

Cell looked at his house on the right. It was in the line of the cannon barrels. "I bet my mom's happy now. Serves her right."

The ambush pine trees were now behind them. There was no turning back.

"How long's it been?" Red said.

"Forty-five minutes," Pal said. The number sounded good.

"So they didn't call the cops," Splinter said.

"How do you know?"

"They'd be here by now."

"And here we are with the potato guns in tote," Red said. He passed the VFW and stopped his truck on side of the road. "We gotta get smarter in case Deep Pockets comes. Splinter, you go take out the cameras, we'll dump the guns and meet you back. If the cops come, then kingdom come. Cell will get a new TV and stuff back. It wasn't us shoot'n off live rounds."

Splinter got out and lumbered off towards the VFW.

Cell stepped out too. "I'll hide the guns," he said.

"What about the hospital report?" Pal asked. "I saw him go down, Red. Do cops monitor those?"

"Dunno," Red said. "Lawyers monitor them for dog bites." He pulled ahead and off the road on vacant land and killed the motor. "Let's work the plan."

Splinter met them at the north end of the fence line and waved them in. They infiltrated the compound and paused in the shadows beyond the tanks.

"That doesn't look good," Cell said, seeing his house down the barrels.

"It's just for show." Splinter said. "Let's go check 'em out."

"Should we wait?" Cell asked.

"Why? Red's getting the tape," he nodded to the door that Red just kicked in. "Camera's are already toast."

"It's been over an hour. They ain't coming back," Cell said. "I'm going to take a look."

Splinter and Cell stood and walked out of the shadow and into the light.

Under halogens mounted on the roof, the VFW parking lot was as bright as day.

"Come on, Pal!" Cell waved and winced in pain. "We're just looking at tanks. Who wouldn't?"

"Besides, they ain't calling the cops," Splinter said again. "Or they'd be here. And they left the fence open."

"Think they're really that stubborn?" Cell turned and asked Pal. "If they are it's perfect!"

"Red's grandfather is," Pal said, stepping into the light. "But he'd kill us all as dead as a turkey-pot-pie if he knew we was messing like this."

"That's all it is," Splinter said. "We're just messing with each other. We're just bored."

Then they stood still.

They were in front of the tanks and gawked.

Red came running up from behind, waving the VHS tape. "Wow!" Red stopped. "They're bigger when you're close."

"Shermans." Splinter said. He was the historian. Pal wiped off some potato and looked at the others. "We better get some bigger guns!" He started laughing, then stopped as he looked at his hand. It was red with blood. He held it up to the others. "I told you I hit one."

The other three leaned in closer and swore. "Is that first blood?" Splinter asked.

"I don't think so," Cell said. "I got shot."

"But no penetration," Splinter said.

"So. I got blood in my pee. That's gotta count, doesn't it?"

Splinter stepped up onto the far tank and looked down the long cannon to Cell's house. Then tugged at the hatch. "This one's locked."

Cell and Red looked up at him. Cell tried to climb but couldn't. His stomach said,'no'.

Pal jumped up on the other. "This one's open," he said. Pal stood on the tank and looked around.

"Mom's gonna be pissed at this," Cell said. "She doesn't like things pointed at her. Serves her right."

"Cover me. I'm going in!" Pal lowered himself half way into the tank.

They looked at him as he held himself up above the opening with his arms.

"Better wait before you come in," Pal said. "Keep a look out." He went down. Once inside, he opened his phone and held it into the dark Sherman to see. "It's been gutted. It's a piece of junk!" he yelled up.

Splinter sat on the turret of the locked tank and looked down at Cell.

Cell leaned by the track, holding his guts with one hand and shook out a cigarette with the other. He held it up to Splinter who reached down from the turret under the flag and took the smoke from the pack.

They were just two gunners on their equipment taking a breather between battles.

A car came from the west and blew by the area.

Red, Splinter and Cell held still and watched the red tail lights fade away.

Then another car came up from the south. It braked at the stop sign and paused. A window came down and a man pointed to the tanks so his children could see them.

Splinter waved.

The man waved back and drove away.

"No one cares," Cell spoke and watched Red climb up on Splinter's tank.

Red made it atop and stretched.

"Whatta ya see down there?" Red asked Pal over the gap between the tanks. All was quiet.

Then the three boys saw movement on Pal's tank and their eyes focused on the upright lid as it tilted, gained momentum and slam shut.

The latch didn't bounce or click. It just sealed as if driven by a great pressure difference.

Red jumped from tank to tank and went to his knees and started pawing, grasping for a handle.

Pal's voice started yelling from inside. It seemed very distant. Very far away.

Splinter and Cell started looking around. Something was wrong.

"Where's the handle on that one?" Red asked Splinter and Cell.

"Right here!" Splinter pointed and touched it.

Red swore and pointed. "It ain't here on this one!"

"Whatta ya mean it ain't there?" Splinter jumped down.

"It ain't here! Whatta ya think I mean!" Red yelled back, swearing.

Cell cocked his head and looked back and forth between Splinter and Red. He sauced the pain and climbed Pal's tank and joined Red. "This ain't good," he said.

"Hey!" Pal found a slide opening and started yelling from where the driver sat. "What's going on? Open the hatch!" He started cussing.

"There ain't no handle!" Splinted swore back. "You're gonna have to open it from inside!"

"There ain't nothing in here to do nothing! It ain't happening from this side."

"This ain't good!" Cell said.

"What'd ya do in there!" Splinter asked Pal.

"Nothing. I just touched this thing and tripped a wire and it slammed shut."

"This ain't good," Cell said, his left hand cupping a black welt on his stomach.

"Use your hands and feel for the handle! How hard can it be?" Red yelled down.

The next few minutes were very long for the topside boys. They scurried around looking for leverage.

"How do you leverage into a tank?" Cell asked.

They started cursing and bumping into each other.

"I'm telling you there's no handle in here! There's no nothing!" Pal yelled from inside. "It ain't happening from in here."

Splinter for the first time knew it was serious. He knew that Red was a redneck and knew stuff about cars and mechanics. He saw Red slowing down and giving up.

"Come on over here." Pal called them to the narrow opening for the driver to see.

They climbed down and came.

"You can stop," Pal said. "I found the trip string. I triggered the hatch."

"I'll be back in a minute!" Cell said and started to run off toward his home. He slowed and walked the rest of the way.

"What's that mean?" Red asked.

"I'm trapped, Red. I walked dead into a trap like a snot-drinking mouse."

Cell returned with a long metal crowbar. His face was white and he was sweating hard despite the cold. "Use this, Red!" Cell said.

Red climbed up and wedged in under the lip of the hatch and started leveraging.

"Get over here and help." Red called.

Splinter came.

Cell couldn't.

"What's going on?" Pal asked.

Cell looked at him. Those atop didn't hear.

Splinter shook his head, "This ain't happening," he whispered to Red. "You don't just pry into a tank."

"Why not?" Red said. "It's sixty years old. Let's get him outta there!" Red swore.

They put all their effort on the long, hexagon pry bar and started cussing. "Cell! Get up here and help!"

Cell grunted up onto the tank.

Splinter, Red and Cell slowly added their weight to the bar. It's hardened tip had a good bit and at just over five hundred pounds of leveraged force, the bar strength gave way and bent under duress.

Cell lifted the crooked bar. "This is serious," he said, looking around.

"Get some help!" Pal echoed from in the metal cocoon and sounded as if he were far underground.

"You know what this is?" Cell whispered to Splinter. After they made eye contact, they looked around.

Cell opened his palms, "We can't get him out and we can't call for help without the cops sniffing around."

"No cops!" Pal yelled from in the tank. He was in the dark but he could still hear. He could see too. He saw the face of a veteran of World War Two pointing a German Lugar at him right after filling Cell with lead. He saw that the soldier didn't care that he had just killed.

And Pal saw the killer's friend reel in impact from his potato.

Inside the dark tank, Pal sat down. He knew retribution was coming his way from men who knew the meaning of the word. And he knew he couldn't run or squeal. He knew then that he was a prisoner of war.

From a quarter mile down the road, tucked in an area just past a streetlight, I turned my truck light on high beam. Me, Ned, Webb and Beans had been talking and laughing for some time. I pulled out onto the road and three boys soon looked our way. That got us chuckling all the more.

The hospital had kept Wendell overnight for observation so he was in good hands. He was going to like this story. He was going to like it a lot.

I pulled out onto the road, gained speed then slowed as the three boys looked at us from atop of Webb's gutted tank.

Seeing them empty handed, I braked, coasted through the four way stop and then turned left into our parking lot.

Those boys leaped behind the turret. They weren't the first to take cover behind an M4.

"There's just three all right," Beans said. "Is that okay, Webb?"

"One's good enough. We only need one for leverage."

Idling up to the tanks I kept the highbeams on them and heard my back left window sliding down. Out my windshield, we saw heads pop out from behind the turret.

Ned was behind me and yelled. "Looks like you lost a man!"

Webb saw into the driver slot of his gutted tank.

A pair of wide eyes were peering out as if Gullom himself had been caged.

Webb smiled.

"How's that potato taste?" Cell yelled back.

Inside the tank, Pal cringed. Cell shouldn't have said that.

Ned brought the window up and I drove past the tanks, circled as tight as my truck allowed, then gained speed for the exit.

What looked like a bent crowbar bounced off my front quarter panel and I knew it left a good dent. But it didn't matter. Michigan white tail deer do all sorts of damage.

We left those kids and sped off into the night, closing the gate behind us with the remote.

"How's he's gonna get out?" Beans asked.

"He can't," Webb said.

"They gotta be the stupidest lads I've ever seen!" Ned said. "There ain't no way we were ever that stupid."

"I met a veteran of the Civil War once," Webb said.

"What did you do?"

"I was only ten," Webb said.

"I bet you didn't disrespect him," Ned said.

Webb shook his head. "He was as old as time. He scared me silent. He scared me still."

"Different times," Beans said.

"What are we gonna do when they start throwing stuff at us besides potatoes?" I asked.

Our smiles left.

"We'll wait them out," Webb said. "Cops will get involved soon enough after that one comes up missing."

"Better yet," Beans said. "We'll let Wendell decide. "He's earned it."

We all nodded at this.

I drove on, my headlights eating away the darkness as I dropped off my friends. My future was once again in the hands of a military man.

It was late when I got home. Very late, but I wasn't tired. I hadn't been tired all night.

16
P.O.W.

A night bird, perhaps an owl, turned sharp in the air, breaking sound as it landed in the pines south of the Sherman tanks. Topside the machines, it made the three teenagers turn and peer into the darkness beyond the streetlight.

"What was that?" Cell asked. He swallowed hard, wincing as he did so.

In the front of the M4 was a slide for the driver to see through. A arm could stick out, but not much more.

Red went to the slide and faced Pal. A weird honor surfaced now that the boys could see each other. Red handed Pal his five D-Cell, black truck flashlight.

"You guys gotta get out of here," Pal said.

"You should be more worried about yourself," Red said.

"Why? I'm inside a tank! What can they do to me?"

After a few minutes the truth came out. "You'll have to cut the hatch with a butane torch," Red said.

"Can't you?"

"It'll be inches think if we come in from the outside. Take hours. The fire will wake everybody up. You'll have to do it. But I don't know if I can hand it to you. This slide's too small."

"Okay," Pal said.

"Tell him the bad part," Cell said.

"I'm not even sure you can do it from in there," Red said. "It'll eat up all your air. Does it stink inside?"

"Yeah. Slippery too."

"Smells like you're sitting in old oil and jack. Sparks could catch your floor on fire. Don't use your lighter." "Better get me a sleeping bag too," Pal said.

The others looked around then at their feet. One of their own had fallen. Splinter and Cell left and sacked the TV house and snuck over some blankets, pillows and food and stuff them into the small hole.

"Don't worry," Splinter said. "We'll think of something.

"What about school tomorrow?" Pal asked Red.

"What of your mom?" Red said.

"Right."

"Write a suicide note and we'll stash it in you room when she's at work," Cell said.

Red smacked him in the head. "Write a runaway note. Tell her that life in Pocketville stinks and you're outta here for a week. How you're gonna thumb to, where's your farthest relative?"

"California," Pal said.

"Perfect."

"She won't go for it," Pal said. "She knows it ain't me."

"Tell her you've changed."

Pal looked around the inside of the tank. Change might work. He was changing by the minute. "Hand me some paper and pen."

In the pre-dawn dark, the skirmish between the old men and young ones became a war.

Wendell, WWII Medal of Honor and recipient of two Purple Hearts, woke up. He proceeded to pull the plug on his monitors. He hated those things. He took also took out his I.V. and did his very best to frustrate every nurse on the floor. If he wasn't butt naked he would have left the place. After he wore out the staff, he fell back asleep.

Peace returned to the nursing station.

But in his sleep the wadding in his mouth loosened and the blood started flowing. He coughed some of it up, then turned on his side and got snoring again.

A drowsy nurse walked by and heard him snoring. "Finally," she said, and never broke stride.

But Wendell's blood kept flowing.

Being on anti-coagulates that slowed his body from producing Vitamin K, a necessary ingredient for blood to scab, didn't help. He had been on the med for the better part of a decade because of a small stroke.

Wendell died in sleep on a pillow soaked in his own blood.

Wendell was 82.

The injury report showed that he had fallen into a metal railing after a poker game at his VFW and opened a deep gash in his mouth. It showed that he received the injury when he was among war buddies at the post.

"A good way to go!" One of the doctors said, looking over the morning report. "Let's treat this man with respect." There was no mention or suspicion, negligence or foul play.

Men get old and die. The lucky ones at least.

The nurses stewed around a bit when asked why his monitors were unplugged.

But then the supervisor spoke to the night shift.

"He was 82," he said.

A dozen or so miles north, in a very tight space, Pal was curling in pain, rolling in diesel and oil that grimed floor of the tank. After downing a 2-liter of Mountain Dew, he now realized there was no place to pee. He couldn't reach the slid, which was near the ceiling and so he had to face the fluid. He urinated on the floor of the tank and spent the rest of early morning wishing he hadn't chucked the bottle outside the hatch hours before.

Pal slept in his stink.

It was a cold dawn, true to the harsh ones that come the month before Easter. The sky showed signs of red in the east, but gray soon covered over all color and day broke.

I looked out my window and saw a few inches of new fallen snow and made the calls.

We met an hour later at the VFW.

Frank's widow and Webb's wife had fixed up muffins and coffee and then sat back and whispered from the corner.

We all laid out our dress uniforms, preparing to pay Wendell respect at the death room at the hospital downtown.

We looked at our stuff, dusted off our pants and coats, polished boots and brass, and lifted our heavy holsters, laden with well-oiled .45's.

Webb jammed a heavy clip into the butt of his weapon. "Battles and witches!" he said out of respect.

The two women looked at him, then looked at each other. Frank's widow nodded.

"They always been this heavy?" I asked.

Webb looked at Ned and Beans. "They're for emergencies. We ain't going to murder no children."

"They're the same age as most the soldiers we killed the last year in Germany," I said.

"This is different," Webb said, nodding to the blank monitors recently sabotaged. "These are American kids. I'll go to the grave potato gunned like Wendell before I kill another kid."

All was quiet as we looked at each other. Then we heard a voice. A far distant voice calling out to us.

Frank's widow heard it too. She put fingers to her mouth.

"Our prisoner is outside cussing, Lefty?" Beans asked.

"A little," I said. "He doesn't like the M4 anymore than we did when we were going against the Tigers."

Ned chuckled. "Remember seeing our 177's bounce off?"

"Nothing like getting the Krouts yelling at you for scratching their paint before inspections." I said.

"Krouts sure loved their inspections."

"Upsetting their inspections was good fun," Ned said.

"Tigers sure shook the earth," Webb said, looking to the door and the sound of an engine.

A horn sounded.

It took us a while, but we all made it to the door, walking by our women who huddled in the corner.

It wasn't right that our women had to huddle in corner. It wasn't right that they were afraid.

Of course Webb and Beans had their hardware out. Big .45's were enough to scare any God-fearing soul.

I shoved open our red, white and blue door and saw two boys in a truck outside our gate.

"Let our friend out!" A boy yelled from his truck window. I motioned for them to turn off the engine.

They did.

Wendell and Bean stepped from behind me, .45's at their sides, the scary ends pointing to the steps.

"They don't know," I said.

"Tell them," Ned said.

"Why you all dressed up?" The driver swore again. They were a good ways off, but it was a quiet morning and only a few cars were commuting workers.

"He's dead."

"Who's dead?" the voice came from the tank.

"You boys killed our friend." I said. "A winner of the Medal of Honor. He died last night."

"You let our friend go!" the driver persisted from the roadside. "Or you'll be sorry."

"You bring our friend back from the dead and we'll let your piss-ant peon go free. Fairs fair!" Webb yelled back.

Guns drawn, Ned and Beans came out from behind me. Webb took the flank by the tank. I stepped forward too and let the door slam behind me. There was no back up in any of us.

A metal clang came from the tank.

We looked.

"You're gonna rot in there!" Webb yelled to the prisoner.

The tank was quiet. We saw fingers withdraw into the darkness of the shell.

Movement in the truck caught our eye. The shaggy blond boy had his body out the far window and was looking at us over the roof of the truck. "You want the world to know your friend died from a potato gun? Winner of the Medal of Honor, dishonored by a Pocketville punk with a basement built potato gun?" the boy yelled this in awkward voice. A troubled one. "I'll spill the story, I swear I will unless you let him go!" Splinter yelled.

"I see every move you make," a voice yelled from the tank. "We'll always know when you're here!"

At this, Webb turned and walked to the tank.

An arm reached out as if to snag him and yank him in, but Webb expected that.

The lads in the truck watched.

Beans and Ned kept their eyes on the truck, ready to blow holes in it if someone twitched.

I looked at Webb and saw the red stick. I turned away quick.

Webb dragged the flare on the tank, blew the seal and ignited a red fire as bright star fire. Diverting his eyes, he thrust the flare towards the slide until the prisoner retreated to the backside of the tank.

Then he dropped the flare into the slide and pulled the slide shut and wired it closed with a metal wire that was attached to it.

We didn't know what to say to that.

Webb came back, blinking only a little. We just looked at the truck and waited for Webb's eyes to get back to normal.

"He can watch us all he wants to now!" Webb spoke to the truck. "But we'll all look like darn toot'n, sun spots for a few weeks!"

The boys in the truck just gave us the finger and roared off. The front tires jerked hard as he overshot his turn. He was seeing spots too.

We looked at Webb and then at the tank. Smoke was pouring out the exhaust vent.

"I don't remember no flare smoking that much," I said.

It ain't the flare," Webb said. "I looks like it caught the oil on the floor on fire."

We turned and looked at Webb.

He looked to us. "She needed to be cleaned out anyway."

Smoke poured from the seams in the tank.

"Think they'll go to the cops?" Ned asked.

"There ain't no way they'll do the joint to save a prisoner." Webb said. "They premeditated. It'd be Murder One."

"What if they do?" I asked.

We were walking to our tanks.

"You want to risk killing our prisoner?" Ned asked.

"What would Wendell want?" Webb asked. "Oh. That's right! We can't asked him!" Webb unhooked the wire and opened the slide. Smoke poured out and we listened to a boy coughing up his lungs.

"You got a Medal of Honor," I looked at Beans. "You decide."

Ned and Webb looked at Beans. It was pinned on his dress coat for the first time. The Medal of Honor.

"You won the Honor!" Webb gawked.

We all went quiet. It was true.

Beans glared at me. He was a man who liked his secrets and I knew it was hard for him to bring it out.

"It's for Wendell," Bean said. Beans was the only one in the area besides Wendell who had won the medal. He won it at Iwo Jima. He knew the price.

"Wendell would want us to win the war!" Beans said, holstered his sidearm and walked away. We followed.

In the distance, three boys were lounging by the big red pick-up in front of the TV house across the way.

Above was a white sky. The frost of night was thawing away. Snow had already melted off the tanks. Smoke still billowed from the one. It would be that way for another ten minutes.

I put my hand over my eyes to help see the smoke coming off the tank. But it was a green blur just the same. But I could hear. I can hear just fine.

"Poor Mr. Potato Head!" the boy in tank yelled to us. Then he coughed hard and long.

I cringed.

The boy's face appeared in the slot below the turret and he was coughing out red phlegm.

Webb stopped walking away from the tank. He turned and went back to it.

The boys in the open across the no man's land street stood up like ground hogs.

Beans stood at our door beyond the ramp, glaring through the fence.

Me and Ned stopped in the middle of the compound and for some reason merged over and took cover behind the rock under the flag. Something was happening. My long gone hand hurt. We turned and looked at Webb. That kid should keep his mouth shut, I thought. That kid should know that. Shut up when you're a P.O.W.

Webb pulled himself up onto the smoking tank. Once balanced, he pulled a string of red-looking cigars from his pocket. His other hand flicked a lighter.

A coated green string sparkled in the overcast air and we watched Webb drop them down the air intake for the motor.

We didn't really hear the dull thunder claps, but we felt the jolts. They stung our old bones. And me and Ned were a good distance away. We looked at the tank.

Webb still had his hands over his ears.

We knew that boy wasn't going to be talking too much smack anymore. Or hearing too much for that matter. Wasn't going to be seeing anything either.

At that point we didn't even know if he was alive. Something came over us then. It was happening. We didn't care either way. We were changing back to what we used to be. We were regressing.

Webb walked back to us.

Beyond Beans the enemy scrambled.

"What was that?" I asked.

"What?" Webb asked.

"What you dropped in the tank?" I nodded to the smoking tank

"Some firecrackers!" his voice was too loud.

We watched the blue, red and black smoke drift out of the tank slide and heard a kid coughing and crying out for help.

I looked back at Webb. "Firecrackers my fusebox!"

"Got any more?" Ned asked.

Webb smiled, not hearing a word.

17
ATTACK / COUNTERATTACK

Police Chief Tabbs was northbound on a winding road that tried to follow the river that cut his town in two. The meeting with his men finished late and his stomach was growling from where it was tucked behind his 40 inch black leather belt. It crunched in on his uniform but allowed his police issue sidearm to ride well on his right hip.

He didn't like to carry a sidearm, being the Chief and all, but he thought it good prudence because a younger officer had a run in with the old timers on the north perimeter on his watch. He knew he couldn't go toe to toe with the grumps up at their VFW, but he wasn't afraid to go hammer to hammer either. Besides, up that-a-way was Triple T. You couldn't be too careful going into the Trailer Trash Territory near Sheriff Soil.

When the road straitened he saw the tanks. Braking, he turned wide only to be confronted by a gate and the formable pose of two tanks pointing their cannons over his hood. He stepped out of his car and skirted a puddle and looked up and down the fence.

"The cops are here!" I said as if we had stacks of cash to hide.

"Deep pockets?" Ned asked.

Wendell and Beans holstered their weapons and nodded.

"It's Tabbs." I spoke over my shoulder and stepped outside on the ramp. The air tasted cold and gray. "You better hide the Thompson," I said and let the door close. In front of me were the tanks and I knew the enemy beyond the roadway took it all in. My Evreaus hand nerved up.

Webb joined me, then stepped in front. He pointed to the fence, palming a garage door opener and clicked it. We heard the chain grind open the gate.

He had the right to speak to the Chief over the rest of us because he paid the tickets.

"Morning Chief," Webb said.

"Morning. Cap'n here?" He admired our full dress uniforms. "You boys getting ready for a parade?"

Beans came strolling out of the door. Brass shining.

"What you boys up too?" Chief asked.

"Going to the hospital to say our respects," Beans said.

"I hadn't heard. What happened?"

"We lost a friend last night." Beans said. He was a customer. No more, no less. No need to cause suspicion.

"Who?"

"A good friend," Beans said and looked beyond the man.

"Hadn't heard."

"Why would you?" Beans said.

"Wendell was 82," I said. That seemed to say it all.

"What do you got here?" he pointed and we strolled over to the tanks.

I leaned on the tank and noticed the slide was open and eyeballs were tucked in there in the darkness.

Webb brushed off some mud. "These are tanks," he said.

"I know that. Why are they here?" Chief nodded. His eyes went down the long barrel of the 177 as he observed the relics.

"I needed to free up some space in my barn," Webb said.

"And the fence and gate?"

"Just to keep the kids off them. Safety first and all," Webb said.

"Good thinking." Chief said. "How'd they get here?"

"The usual," Webb said.

Chief looked to the road and saw the carvings in the asphalt.

"D.O.T. going to get you for that," he pointed.

"How they going find out?" Beans asked.

"What's that sulfur toilet smell?" Chief asked.

"What smell?" I asked.

"Is it a rat?" Beans asked.

"Funny," Chief said. "You must be the one hasseling my officer."

"I think that was him," Ned pointed to Webb.

"Could be anything," I said. We watched Chief circle the tanks, dragging his fingers across the steel.

Tabbs took a step closer to the Sherman with the prisoner.

I looked at Ned who gave me a strange signal.

"You keep them locked up?"

"What for?" Webb asked. "It's pretty quiet around here?"

The slide of the tank was open and Chief leaned and peered into the darkness.

"Careful Chief," Webb said. "Some tomcats crapped in that one something fierce last winter. Stunk my whole barn up. Webb stepped forward and slid the slide shut. "I better keep that closed so others don't come after the scent.

All was quiet.

"Smells like you smoked them out." Chief asked.

"Of course."

"You kill them?"

"That's illegal," Webb said.

"Cats and rats are apart of God's creation," Beans said. "We just can't go around killing them, despite what they do."

"These tanks really drive here from your place? That's two miles of road damage!"

Webb and I looked at the tread tracks and some shredded asphalt stuck to them from the road.

"Drove 'em in at night on the road shoulder," Webb said. "We're setting up a museum of sorts to help educate Pocketville children. After the flag ordeal it seemed the right thing to do."

Chief smiled. "If DOT finds out it didn't come from me."

Beans smiled back. He didn't buy it.

After some chit and chat, Chief Tabbs left, saying the department would be making a donation to Wendell's charity. He drove away and the slid whipped open and we saw the boy's oil stained face. Hair above is eyes seemed singed a bit.

"You missed your chance, boy." I taunted, standing by the tank track, then I remembered he couldn't hear.

Webb never saw it coming. A soft brown turd came from the tank slide and struck his trousers, leaving a brown smudge.

"Smell that! You old Nazi!" a boy yelled from in the tank. Normally a lad to weigh decisions, Pal was now off balance. The bleeding from his left ear had stopped, but with his equilibrium gone, he had to move about on his hands and knees because the torch seemed to have burned his eyes. He wrecked out his blanket when he smothered it.

What Pal wanted know was a fight. A chance to get in the open. Once outside, he could outrun them. He could outrun them all. Even Red, Splinter and Cell.

Webb looked at his pants.

"That's crap on your dress uniform," Ned said.

Beans went to the Post and dragged back the hose. "A little cold water will get that off," he said.

Too late. Webb drew his .45 and pointed it inside the hole. He wasn't the type to fire a .45 into the hole just to listen to the slug bounce around until it sunk into someone's hide. But these were trying times and his fishing buddy had just been killed.

We all knew what a flattened slug would do to a turd tosser.

It was Webb's decision. He knew the bullet would bounce around for about a half mile of geometry as it searched for something soft. He pulled pieces of men out of tanks before.

Webb holstered his weapon and splashed water on his pants from the hose.

I looked at Ned and nodded. Not killing the boy was the right call.

Webb splashed more water on the stain.

"Come in here and get me!" the boy's yell echoed out the narrow slide. It was abnormal loud.

"Let's get him cleaned up!" Webb said.

"What?" the boy yelled.

"That's a good place," Ned said, pointing to the air intake and Webb stuffed in the hose.

"It's nice and high," Beans said. "It'll cool him down too."

"And get rid of that stink!" Webb said and he wedged the hose into the air intake.

"Hey!" the prisoner started yelling and cussing and we four just stood under the flag, listening again to agonizing screams of a child.

"Where did those other three go?" Webb asked Ned.

Ned looked at his watch. "They split after Meal Tab left."

I looked around at the blurs. It would take a good hour for the belly of the tank to fill. After a while it would pour out the viewing slid. "I don't like not knowing where they're at," I said, squinting.

"Let's get going," Beans said. "We're sitting ducks out here."

Webb walked over to where our hose was attached to the VFW and turned her on full tilt.

We then got the women into Webb's truck and locked up the place. We were getting ready to visit our dead friend.

The screams of the prisoner filled the parking lot air as we drove off. Me and Beans followed Webb, Ned and the women.

I could see the women looking at each other in the back seat of Webb's truck. I hoped Ned would settle them down. No telling what a scared woman would say.

That boy wasn't screaming to wake up the earth worms. They were screams of pain. Screams of war. Screams of torture.

Me and Beans got in my truck. "I feel bad for the women," I said. "Hearing things like that can echo for a while."

"They'll get used to it," Beans said, nodding to Webb's truck. "Ned will set them straight."

My uniform creaked from lack of wear as we went on down the road. Beans did too. I wasn't going to be the one to tell him that women weren't predictable.

"His friends better not go too far if they want to save him from his ice age," Beans grunted.

"How cold do you think that water is?" I asked.

"Michigan cold, Lefty. Michigan cold!" Beans said.

"You really think Wendell would want us to hypothermic him?" I asked.

"We can't ask Wendell now can we?" Beans said.

"An eye for an eye makes the whole world blind," I said.

"So, he's already deaf, blind and numb." Beans said. "He's over half way to Helen Keller."

"There's gotta be a better way is all I'm saying. We're smarter than them. We know that no one wins a war."

"They started it." Beans said.

I just kept driving, eyeing my mirror once in a while. That kid was still human, and humans are smart. They'll find a way to hit us and I didn't want to get killed by no punk teenager.

I started thinking about how I could talk some sense into that kid without betraying my brothers.

Inside Pal's black world, he soon gave up plugging the onslaught of water and went to his phone, texted, HELP, and sent it to Red, Splinter and Cell. His right eye was starting to see better. He crawled up onto a metal stand and watched the water rise. As he shivered, he kept losing balance and had to put his hand on the cold metal to balance. He soon went numb. A while later, he stopped shivering.

Then his three comrades came and yanked out the hose. But the cold had gotten inside Pal's bones. He had been in the water.

"The guy who thought of this is really dangerous." Pal yelled out to Red.

"Sorry it took so long. Cops are around and we're thinking they'll ambush."

"What?" Cell asked.

Red repeated, but Pal just looked around, squinting and not seeing anything.

"He can't hear," Cell said. "They blew his ears."

"Hurry!" Splinter said.

"Help me!" Pal pleaded.

"Let's get out of here," Cell said. "They'll come back and get us. We're fools. And these guys don't care if they kill us all."

"You're just saying that cause you got shot," Splinter said. "Let's just help Pal. He's the one in the slammer."

"What!" Pal yelled.

"Here's another phone," Splinter handed in his phone.

"Text only. I can't hear!" Pal yelled.

Red looked at Pal whose face had gone cold white in the iron coffin. He was soaked and numb and the water of war had driven up near the turret.

"Good thing he has a phone," Cell said. "I bet those army guys don't even know he has a phone."

"They know. Cell phones were in Star Trek," Splinter said.

"I don't think they care either way," Red said.

Neither did Pal. His body temp was dropping again.

18

THE MACHINE

By the time I pushed the clicker and opened the gate to the VFW property, the sun had fallen in the west and darkness was rising from the ground itself. I felt hard and bitter. Seeing Wendell with no color took away a piece of me. All of us felt weaker. Older. We didn't have more of each other with him gone. Chesterson was right. We had less. He carried a piece of all of us into the dirt.

Didn't even glance in my rearview mirror at the house behind me that Beans had shot up. I didn't care. I left my F350 running. I hardly ever shut her down anymore. Matter of fact she ran most of January and February this year when I was out and about. She was like me, except she had all her tires.

Walking around the eight foot bed, I pulled out a short hose and walked into the halo of my headlight. Between the dull roar of my engine and the tanks I went and then noticed the hose was on the ground, overflowing the puddles across most of our parking lot. I looked at the exhaust area of the prisoner tank and saw it shine wet in the light. I wasn't alone.

I started feeding the short hose into the air intake of the Sherman only to have it yanked out of my hands as if the machine was inhaling a string of spaghetti. I walked to the slide.

"So your friends rescued you?" I asked the boy locked inside.

A face cussed at me and I turned my head away.

At my truck stood two teenagers. They were as Beans had described.

The chubby tubby stepped to one side and back. More of a retreat than anything.

But I wasn't thinking about that. I focused on the baseball bat in the hands of the skinny kid.

The batter charged and swung an arcing blow with enough spice to bust my nut.

I stepped into it and thrusted my left palm under his armpit and thunked him into the tank with enough hot-sauce to send him to Texas. He got himself hurt.

Good thing too, since I had been on empty for a long time. "What's your name?" I asked, turning my back to the fat one. I felt him walk up but his footfalls came in slow and didn't cause me alarm. I never took my eyes off the Batboy.

He couldn't talk yet, holding his noggin and trying to suck out the pain with his hands like a TV faithhealer. His hand pulled back and it was red with blood. He had some drizzle on his lips.

So I turned to my right and spoke to the fat body in the shadow. "What's your name?"

"Cell," the boy said.

"What do you want with my prisoner?"

"Nothun."

"You his friend?"

"Yea," he said. The one on the ground starting moaning and rolled over to his knees.

"What's the name of the one in the tank?"

"Ask him yourself!"

"He can't hear. We blew his ears out."

"He's Pal," the skinny one said, coming to a stand, then sitting back in the mud, dazed. Blood from the top of his head was now running down his face.

I looked down and him. He was tall if he could get his balance. A good half foot above me. Good thing I cooled him off.

A passing Pocketville Police cruiser saw my truck, spiked his brakes and entered the lot.

"Cell, you get your bleeding friend under the tank," I said.

"It's Deep Pockets!" Cell said and scrambled into the darkness, dragging Splinter into the cold mud under the tank just before the cop spot lit me up.

"Hand out the end of the hose." I spoke hard into the tank slide and smiled when I saw it peep out like an earthworm, shaking to the hypothermic rhythm of the boy inside. Funny how the deaf could now hear.

"Something going on here again?" the officer said. "I see you got your flags straight. We're trying to watch the place better." He walked up shining a metal flashlight tucked back behind his shoulder. I zipped the hose with my thumb pinched over the top and water pouring out. "What's happening?"

I pointed the hose down. "Setting a siphon," I said.

"Vandals?" The officer said, the force was in his voice.

"Kids'll be kids," I said. "Looks like they stuffed the hose into our tank to make a hottub."

"More like a cold tub," the officer rubbed off the night chill.

"Yea. I bet it is pretty cold in there. What are you up to tonight?"

"Me? Nothing. But now because of these stupid brats, I gotta file a report."

"Don't bother. She's a gutted tank. Nothing inside."

"I'll bother. Chief wants me to bother. He likes his reports. And I'll never pass an opportunity to nail a punk."

I nodded to the other tank. "They're just being kids. Just like us back in the day. You can let 'em be. Besides," I nodded to the other tank. "That's our good one. This one just for show."

"Who's us?" The officer had to move away from the pooling water and dropped the light to the ground.

"Us Vets. These are our babies."

"You men get the right permits for these?"

"We're by the book," I said, smiling in the dark.

"Who's hassling you?"

"You know kids nowadays. Pretty harmless." I felt the heavy .45 in my belt. But that was just to keep honest people honest. He didn't need to know about that. "I scared 'em off when I drove in?"

Something clunked from inside the tank and we turned to it. "Water's coming back down now," I said. "She's settling." I turned and started walking to the VFW building. "Better turn off the hose to keep the bills down." We walked over and the deputy did the heavy work, dragging the hose back and coiling it. Idling back to the Shermans, we checked the siphon.

"That'll get 'er done," the deputy said, handing me a card. "Sure you don't want to be named in the report. We don't cotton to trouble makers around here. And I was never like them when I was young."

"No need. We all go astray, but no damage has been done."

"Invasion. Destruction of property!" Oh, I going to make quite a list.

"Doesn't sound to be that truthful."

"Doesn't have to be! We'll make it stick. Do it all the time on less. It's how we stay in business! You want me to knock on the doors around here and get some suspects?"

"You think there's more than one?" I said.

"I'm sure of it. Delinquents always partner. How are your partners doing? Heard you lost one."

"You did huh?"

"Yes. The paper said it happened here."

"It did?" I sensed his suspicion. He wanted a witch hunt for more kids.

"Anything I should know about?"

"Matter of fact there is!" I stepped closer to the tank. In front of me and at my feet were itching ears. I held out the card and read the name. "Officer Dan Mansky, Pocketville Police. They really call you Deep Pockets?"

The officer smiled, "They call us all Deep Pockets," he said. "But what of the accident? What really happened? Those kids had something to do with it! Wait! Even if they didn't we can still link 'em if they were hassling you. It'll be a stretcher, but we've done it before."

"His name was Wendell Cromble. Did four years in combat in the Big War. Won the Medal of Honor, you know."

"I read that," he leaned in. "You know if we get punks into the system it's a black hole. Hotel California stuff! You know what I'm saying? You can check in but you can't check out. Even for the small stuff."

"Why's that?"

"Why's what? Don't worry about that part. Just help me feed the system."

"We're off the record here, right?" I asked.

"Way off!" Deep Pockets stepped in closer.

"Well now you got me interested in Hotel California. That another name for the jail?"

"It's more than that! It's the system. The Status Quo. The Machine. It works like this. They get locked up poor. We let them out poorer."

"Everybody knows that."

"Here's the catch. Get it? After they're out, The Machine makes it tricky to pay off their debts. The county doesn't take most forms of payment when they get released."

"I thought doing time was payment."

"No. No. No. They'll see the judge a couple of times so they get socked with court cost. Nothing big, but around a thousand bucks. Then they got Room and Board cost and some other stuff that goes to the County Clerk. They tack on some cost too. Everybody gets a slice of the fresh meat."

"That so?"

"Here's the kicker. They can't just pay off debt with a credit card, cash or even a personal check. County doesn't take forms of normal currency. Only Certified Checks, which of course a broke person can't get without borrowing cars, opening checking accounts or whatever."

I was turning away. He was losing me and it still didn't seem that tricky.

"Wait," he took hold of my arm and I looked down and his hand until he let go. "You come through for us with some suspects and we'll wipe the mess away! Each agency has a 14 digit routing code that the ex-con has to write on the certified check and each agency needs its own check! It's perfect! There's dozens pieces of pie. How many loser punks have the tenacity to not only get the money, but handle the bureaucracy of transferring routing numbers on dozens of checks to dozens of agencies? And they all go through the Clerk's office so everything's gotta be perfect and uniform. It's impossible. And once they miss payment it like doubles, they can't afford it, so we go and collect them and lock 'em up all over again. And the process starts all over again."

I leaned in. "Now I get the picture! You're not the only one with deep pockets."

"That's right! Now, who do you expect? Is it that fat kid across the street? It's gotta be him. We had his dad so deep we drove him out of the state!"

"The truth is, Deep Pockets, is that old Wendell slipped in our bathroom while taking a piss," I egged him good. "We weren't gonna let that story get out! Not ever! So we decided the fudge the truth a little. So we said he fell on them there steps. We fudged the scene!" I smiled. "You ever fudge an investigation? Or see one of your brothers get hurt shoveling snow and spin it so he threw out his back in the line of duty!" I smiled and elbowed him.

"Ain't that the truth! The beauty of Workman's Comp!" Deep Pockets said. "That's how our world goes around! But I'm telling you straight. If kids were on your property, we can say they messed up your steps and made the man fall. I wouldn't mind whipping some cream up for the punks that did the flag! We could make her stick!" He smiled and clicked off his flashlilght and it seemed to take a minute for our eyes to adjust to the softer, dome light coming down from above our door.

"But that'd be Manslaughter. That just wouldn't be right!"

"Manslaughter? Our Prosecutor would go for Second Degree Murder. She's good. We get scum off the street and keep The Machine going, that's all that counts. Just feed The Machine. You know what I mean? And the P.A. would probably settle out for Manslaughter. Just enough to get family member to file in Civil Court."

"Kind of the like the Krouts stoking the ovens."

"Who?"

"Nevermind," I said. "I'm not about that. That's not how problems are solved in the first place. I'll check with Webb. Maybe he put the hose in himself to clean it out." I held out my hand, nervous now because the rhythmic vibration was happening soft deep in the tank. My prisoner had hypothermia.

We said our goodbye's and I watched him drive off. I saw the baseball bat come into view first as two mud covered shadows stood upright.

I looked in the tank and saw the eyes of a kid called Pal.

We watched the cop car go over the hill.

"Whoa!" Cell said. "We ain't gonna win if we call them. That's for sure." Splinter cussed and rubbed his head.

"You okay?" I asked.

He swore at me and his hands wrangled the bat, thinking hard about another swing.

I was ready to give it to him. I kept my hand by my waist.

"Get back, Splint. He ain't bare handed anymore," a voice in the tank said. "Bare hand," the fat kid corrected.

Splinter was beyond listening. He raised the bat over his shoulder. He chocked up on the grip and I saw his eyes measure the distance between us. For a moment I thought he and I were gonna play some more ball.

So I pulled up my shirt and tucked it behind the .45.

They all saw it.

"I'm done playing baseball with you, boy!" I said. And despite my peaceful talk, I was ready to pull down and get him good. He dropped the bat by opening his hands and it fell to the ground from over his right shoulder.

"What's your name?" Cell asked.

"Lefty." I said.

"How'd to learn to throw someone like that?" Cell asked.

"Those that can't are all dead."

"What's gonna happen to him in the tank? the batter asked, he sounded different."

"He's gonna die."

"And you came to help him?"

"Why'd you come?" I smoked his face with the fire in my voice.

"I'm sorry," the voice in the tank said.

"Your name Pal?" I asked and saw his eyes nod.

"I'm sorry," he said again.

"You the one that killed my friend?"

"Yes Sir," Pal said.

I admired that. Murder ain't easy to admit to. Crime in general isn't. Only a dozen or so of Stalin's Red Army Men pleaded guilty to some two million reported rapes. I'd have liked to seen this Pal kid face to face.

"Go back to my truck and bring those bags of charcoal," I said to Splinter and Cell. They walked away.

"How you doing, prisoner?" I asked.

"Ca co. Cold," he said. More than his breath came out of the slide.

I smelled sixty years of diesel scum and a burnt oil and grime smell from the flare.

"Welcome to war," my eyes iced as I pulled my pistol and pointed it at the boy who killed a Medal of Honor friend of mine. "You keep messing with us and we'll kill you boys off. You send them the message. You surrender. You think you have the most to lose but you don't. You throw yourselves to the mercy of Deep Pockets or we will mercy you!"

Pal nodded. He was a peacemaker now.

The others arrived with the charcoal. "What now?"

"Make a fire under the tank and get his bathtub warm or he won't survive the night."

"What about the cops?"

At this I said nothing. We didn't have anyone to blame for this mess except ourselves.

19

THE FUNERAL

Beans and Webb entered VFW Post 3946 that morning carrying M1A1 Thompsons, the standard infantry rifle of World War Two and the weapons looked oddly out of place because none of the cities or buildings around us had been burned to the ground. Ned came in next. I tilted my head. He carried a very small rifle with a enormous scope resting just above the barrel casing.

"What this?" I asked.

"What?" Beans said. I looked at him.

"It's for our display. We're setting up a display, remember?" Webb said.

Beans grunted and thumped a heavy ammo box on the table, nearly upsetting the balance of things.

"Display my right arm!" I said.

Ned locked the door behind him and scanned the horizons once again. Pulling a long cylinder from his pocket, he screwed it around the end of his little rifle. Holes had been drilled into the cylinder, so stuffing in the barrel would absorb cartridge gases. I didn't ask why he had a silencer. I didn't have to. Webb, Beans and Ned were going to kill those other three children.

"Only three to go," Beans said.

I looked outside. A light snow had fallen last night and they hadn't noticed the tanks. "I think there's still four."

"Get over it, Lefty. He's dead."

"He's alive," I said, looking out the window in the kitchen. I didn't know what bothered me worse. Knowing there was a tortured kid encased in one or our tanks freezing to death, or knowing my three friends thought he was inside floating face down in the oil and diesel sludge.

They came alongside and looked.

"That's strange," Webb said. Snows been melted off my prisoner tank."

Ned brought his rifle down and blinked. "They built a fire underneath it and kept him warm. Smart. It's how we got the diesels going during the cold times."

"Maybe they cooked him instead," Beans said.

I looked at Webb and Beans. Ned was gone. That got me nervous too. Ned's always been good in the bush. But with him and his pet rifle thumping around up in the crawl space of some bell tower, things could get plum dangerous.

I decided not to tell them about last night.

"Look!" Webb pointed and opened the window. We watched from deep inside the VFW, behind locked doors and a heavy fence.

Smoke and spark danced and popped from under the tank.

From in the attic crawl space, Ned had ascended and was drilling the coal fire under the Sherman. At every bullet whistle of his .22 rifle, more ash and heat exploded from the pile."

"Resilient," I said.

"We have to hand it to them," Webb said.

"We'll hand it to them soon enough," Beans said. "But first we'll pay respects to the dead."

"Those boys ain't no threat while we got a live one," I said. "Might as well deal some cards." We went and sat.

Then we heard the scream. Not a normal one. It was of terror and disbelief and came to us from across the street. Us three looked across the table.

Beans kept the cards coming. We watched five of cards spin into a pile where Ned was to sit.

Webb looked towards the door. "Nobody thinks it can happen to them the first time," he said.

Then we heard footsteps on the attic ladder.

Ned was back.

Fifteen years ago, when Red's parents had gotten divorced, his mom wiped out his dad financially because he always went hunting on court dates. But the dad got custody, because she knew the man would kill her if she took his kid. Red's mom went on to build up a decent veterinary clinic at the north end of town, then died and few years back and left the whole thing to her business partner, Berta.

Berta wasn't socialable.

Red knocked on her clinic door, then looked around. Cars on the road seemed to be going slower than normal. He felt they were watching him. But it was desperate times.

Seeing Splinter slumped in his truck scared him to knock again. Harder. He was hoping Berta would remember him. He had been in and out of the clinic a few times. Once when he needed an X-Ray to see if he had a concussion and twice for stitches. Maybe a few more time for some antibiotics when his nasal infections got the best of him.

Red missed his mom. She could fix anything, but this time it was different. He was glad she was gone and Berta was doing the deed.

She opened the clinic door. "What happened?" She asked. "You look fine."

"I'm Red. You remember me?"

"Of course. Your mom talked about how much you hated her after she stacked up felonies to help you," Berta spoke, her face staying round and expressionless.

Red backed up, expecting the door to slam. It wasn't going good. "We need some help," Red said. He looked behind and into the Waiting Room where a lady sat with a cat. The cat looked at him. Cats always know.

"Come on in and get in line," Berta said. "What's your Pet's name."

"Splinter," Red said. "His name is Splinter."

"What is he?"

"I think we better use the back door," Red said.

She moved her body around Red and saw into the truck.

A white faced boy met her eyes and lifted a hand, bandaged in a blood soaked rag.

Berta looked around.

That's a good sign, Red thought.

"Drive him around back," Berta said, closing the door on Red.

Red obeyed and he and Cell dragged Splinter inside and laid him flat onto a stainless table where his clothes soaked up some pooled animal blood.

Berta entered. "What happened?" she snapped on some gloves and depressed a syringe into a clear bottle then pulled it out and tapped the bubble up, squirting liquid into the air from the needle. "It's a felony to have you here so fess up or walk out!" she said, pouring some iodine into a bowl by Splinter's wound and preparing to inject the needle into the bloody pulp.

"It's a felony for us too. So I guess that makes us even!"

"We ain't even. You get those cat traps away from old man Jones down the road and we'll be even. He traps everyone's pet then throws 'em on the road and runs over them a couple of times to make it look like an accident. You git 'im and we'll be even," Berta said.

"Deal," Cell said.

"So what'd you do, Splinter?" Berta asked. "Get too close to the cookie jar?"

Red looked at Cell and Splinter. He wished Pal was here. Pal was good at reading people's character to see what their motive was. Instead, Red just spilt the truth.

"We're the ones messing with the Veterans. You know. The Nazi flag thing. He went on to explain their war.

Berta listened, then started working on Splinter.

By the time Red finished, she had the wrappings off, numbed up the area and had it cleaned off. "Sounds like they're messing with you boys more than you're messing with them."

Red never mentioned the potato guns. He sorta left that out.

She pulled thread through a bent needle. "No turning back on this. Sure you don't want the finger?" she asked. "You can go public and maybe they can stick it back on if you can find it. It's pretty cold out."

Splinter shook his head, "Just stop the bleeding," he said.

Cell walked to the door and stood by it. The room was warm and he had started sweating under his Kevlar, now an essential part of his wardrobe.

"This is good enough for me. It is just pinky after all!" Splinter said.

She handed the thread and fishhook looking needle to Red. "You'll need to know how to do this," she said.

Red took the suture equipment.

Splinter looked at him and nodded. The nub was numb anyways.

Cell walked up to get a better look.

"Welcome to being a soldier!" Berta said. "Stab in right about there and let's get 'er going."

Red looked into the eyes of his friends. "It's happening dudes! We're doing a field dressing."

Splinter closed his eyes.

"Next time you won't need me," she said and walked out of the room.

Ned's wife and Frank's widow pooled their experience and prepared the funeral details. It was a ceremony of celebration of the life of Lieutenant Wendell Filmore.

Sixty three veterans attended. But those involved in the procession details were the great ones. The ones that saved the world. The local National Guard would by firing a six gun salute, a special honor reserved for those who earned the Congressional Medal of Honor.

Police Chief Tabbs had cruisers prepared at the road crossings to stop traffic. Pocketville's Mayor Belanny would be presenting the outline of the soldier's life. He lost his father in the Great War.

A low, quiet and constant murmur reverberated around Moaner's Funeral Home from the attendees as the open coffin displayed a man of honor. It was a proud day for Pocketville and its Veteran's of Foreign Wars chapter. Even the shadow members of the club had been seated in dress uniform, but they were nothing compared to the stoic figures of Wendell's four surviving comrades who were decorated in full combat gear, including pistols holstered under their leather folds and rifles slung across their shoulders.

The surviving four World War Two veterans showed honor well. People looked at them with respect and awe as they stood abreast their fallen friend among the flowers and photographs.

All the who's who of Pocketville were there. And by and large is was a silver haired group that crowded the funeral home except for Duke Dungy, who was flashing photographs and getting people lined up in pose.

Then they entered.

I saw them first.

Red, Splinter and Cell approached and the doors closed behind them because they were the last. A few people turned as the doors clicked shut. Murmurings increased.

Mayor Belanny started making his way forward from a group where he had been pumping handshakes.

The boys were wearing black suits and Splinter's hand was in a sling inside a suit coat. His sleeve was empty like mine.

I coughed and turned my back to Webb and the crowd, stepping in front of Beans and Ned.

Ned was cool but the face of Beans and Webb flushed in blood. It was in the eyes of Beans. Just a raw meanness so I stayed with Webb. He was shaking and I didn't want there to be a scene because Wendell's family was up in front and his older sons, both in their fifties, were in mourning.

Webb went to push me but I stood my ground. "You let it go for Wendell!" I hissed

"Lefty," Ned started whispering into my ear. I herd his .45 holster casing snap open. Now me and Webb looked at Ned.

The boys were about sixty odd years younger than anyone else the crowd and got the attention.

We watched them come up the aisle like sinners to God's alter.

By Gerry or Jew, Beans was first in line to greet them.

"Maybe it's over," Ned said. "They probably have extra coffins here too."

I looked over to the Pocketville officers at the door. We had to pay overtime for them to handle traffic.

The three lads approached and passed us and went to the coffin.

We soon found out the truth.

Each pulled out and potato and rested them along Wendell's body inside the coffin. Then they faced us and did a half way decent salute. They even held it until Beans saluted and released them.

Splinter lingered on for a moment, something was behind his eyes and I stepped forward.

He paused and reached out his left hand for me to shake.

That was going too far and I stepped passed his outstretched hand and took hold of the hand in the sling under the coat. The other two were already in stride and walked off to find seats.

Beans, Ned and Webb stepped between Splinter and his friends, blocking any rescue. Divide and conquer. Keep is simple stupid.

"How have you been, son?" I asked.

Maybe the first two rows could hear if normal whispering was going on. But all had stopped. It was dead still and all watched and heard.

"Are you doing okay, son?" I asked again and people sensed that they may be in the presence of something special.

Splinter was a cool customer and just nodded, clenching his teeth to hold the scream inside.

"You sure you're okay, lad? Times like this are so tough!" I gave his nub a good joint of electricity and his eyes bulged and exploded in tears.

A muffled scream eeped out but he choked off by pain and grit.

Most of the crowd nodded in sympathy for the grief of the young man.

By then his two idiot friends knew they'd been flanked and stopped. They wanted to come back but Beans stepped in front of them, blocking their way to the casket and Splinter's aid.

Ned was there, ever the doctor and hand a hand of counsel on the lad's shoulder.

All the dull mutterings throughout the funeral home had ceased and it was dead still out of respect for the boy who seemed to be taking Wendell's death very, very hard. Good thing those two old veteran were with him. The one armed man was helping the boy with his emotions, even holding the boy's slung hand. They've always been such a giving generation.

I grunted as I clamped down on Splinter's de-pinky'd hand. I felt a slimy wetness come between my hand and his, but I never lost my grip. Not even close.

Tears were across his face and coming off his chin now. His knees shook and his cheeks were rippling as if facing a wind tunnel. He eeped a chirp of pain for the entire room.

I turned him to the audience and nodded to Duke Dungy, who flashed a picture of the lad between me and Ned. That one was going to be framed above were Wendell sat.

Wendell would like that.

Splinter turned back to me and started going light on his feet. "Please," he whispered as if I were ringing his

Rocky Mountains. He seemed ready to collapse as he rested his head on my shoulder.

"We all miss him," I said, seeing many widows in the room nod in unison. I squeezed off another round of pressure on the his wound and the boy winced in agreement.

So focused on Splinter's suffering was the crowd that no one saw Beans.

No one but the two boys. The fat one and the red one. They stood by the wall facing their friend.

Beans was in front and Webb was to the right of Beans, sheltering the man from the audience.

Webb did a double take at Beans and nearly stopped him, but he was too awed to do anything.

So were the boys. They just stared at Beans.

Around the neck of Beans was a string of leather. It was a thick one like a hunter would use to tie his boots. On the string hung the finger of Splinter. Beans wore it like a trophy. No surprise there. Ned and Webb helped make the necklace.

But as the boys watched Splinter being tortured and felt a surge of energy to rescue him, they noticed the small man in front of them. They saw what he was doing and it back them up.

But they were pulled to him nevertheless. Maybe their eyes were playing tricksey.

Beans had taken the finger in his hand and had raised to his teeth. He then started chewing the meat and skin off finger, exposing more of the bone for the boys with every bite.

Ned and Lefty and many others grieved with the lad.

"Just let it out, Son," Ned said as I crunched down on his juicy knuckle, but there was no more energy left in the boy to fight.

Veins in Splinter's neck bulged. It wouldn't be the first head I'd seen pop off. I ran over people in tanks before.

"Funeral's of loved one's are so hard. Can we help you with anything?" Ned asked.

Women were bringing up white handkerchiefs to dab their eyes upon seeing the lad's grief.

I let him go and Ned caught him so he didn't collapse.

Ned extended his arm, leading the distraught boy to the safety of his friends, who had all but forgotten him.

The wounded kid joined his friends and they were seated. Splinter was soon rocking back and forth holding the hand and searching for relief.

Funerals are tough times.

Ned pulled a handkerchief from his pocket as Bean's hand went to my shoulder.

Beans seemed proud of all forms of cruelty.

I turned my back to the crowd and faced Wendell one final time as I wiped blood from my hand. Then I saw in on the floor. Dozens of drops of blood were in the carpet. I smeared them with my foot and dropped the stained handkerchief into Wendell's casket over the potatoes. Nice touch.

He would like that.

Police Chief Zimmer got up and stood next to the mayor, nodding to the gathering that it was beginning.

"We welcome all who gather for respects and to mourn," he said.

People nodded and the old women took the hands of their men.

In the middle row of the funeral service was Knoxal, and beside him was Brance, the elder worker from Pocketville Hardware. Brance leaned over to his boss. "Mourn and respect gots nothing to do with those potatoes."

20

Fire and Truck

In the days following the funeral of Wendell, the big mud puddle around the Sherman tank smelled of oil, diesel and sewage as Pal the prisoner settled into his confinement.

His friends snuck him dry blankets, food and water. We let them. Maybe we were going soft.

Webb spent his days tinkering on his toys.

Beans and Ned went down to Ohio fulfill some details of Wendell's will.

I tended the prisoner as to the rules of the Geneva Convention. "How's the ringing?" I asked once, we were alone.

"Gone. But my left ear is dead. It's stopped bleeding."

"Nothing but noise pollution out here anyways," I said. "You'll get used to it."

"What?" the prisoner asked.

"I asked if you going to miss your Rock–n-Roll?"

"I don't listen to that kind of music," Pal said.

I just looked at him through the slide. Then I looked around. Was I outliving Rock-n-Roll?

I didn't visit him the same time everyday because I was wary of his allies. I knew what they would do with me. I knew what they did with Wendell. I kept to the back side of the tank and carried iron. It would take a heck of a shot to bring me down.

"How's the funeral?" he asked.

"Gripping," I said and I told him about the squeeze. After I finished with Beans and the finger, Pal drifted back in the darkness. No surprise there, I was the one who said being deaf and blind had its advantages.

Rain roared in sideways the next day but as the front passed it settled into a steady drizzle. Me and Webb didn't care either way. It was a warm rain, coming in from the south with some lightning. It gave us cover. Not from the punks.

Ned gave us that.

We we're now worried about Knoxel and Brance at Pocktetville Hardware. They seemed to want to horn in.

I secured Webb's muscle hooks and cable around the base of one of the sixty footers. About a dozen of those pine trees were good size. It took an hour for the Sherman to uproot the biggest. We broke them down. Most forest are no match for tanks.

Webb had short cables too, and we used them to loop the bigger trees to his main cable. With the soil being sandy, it drained well despite some mud patches. And most of the remaining trees were shorter. We just crushed them under the tank tracks and used the big cabled trees to snag up the small ones and corral them into a big pile.

The engine roared, but once the tracks got the weight moving it was over. We watched the toppled trees get grouped.

The ground shook and we were men. It took us two hours. Working slow and smart, the tank uprooted and moved the forty odd trees into a pile in the middle of the field. Tanks sure made mowing a forest an easy thing. It pushed them high and we dumped gallons of diesel, pouring it from Webb's square jerry can onto old tires.

"That'll get her going." I said after Beans tossed in a couple of flares to wake things up. Smoke billowed in the wind and rain.

Wiping our hands, me and Beans stepped closer to be warmed by the fire. "Rains washing the mud off," Webb said, panting from climbing out and down from the tank.

I nodded, winded. "What's next?" I knew if I asked the question it sounded like I could handle the cards. And truth the tallied, I felt like Wendell had reached up and grabbed hold of me.

Beans stepped up and dropped a heavy horseshoe and pin onto the back of the Sherman.

"Now we park her and grate," Webb said.

Once warmed, we climbed aboard and Webb tanked us back to the VFW. Crossing the street, we made a SUV brake.

That driver just looked at me and Beans sitting on the tank. It was like old times, except I didn't shoot him.

Back on the V.F.W. we washed the mud, grass and wood shreds from the tank and noticed the arrival of Red's big 4x4 truck at the fat kid's TV house.

Ned came out and told us to be cautious because noses were pressed to the window, but we weren't the type to leave any job half baked.

We looked south and saw the fire growing to forty feet. A thick, black smoke was coming our way. It was a bad smell, hinting of long dead fires that burned human flesh.

Webb finished fiddling in the tank, peeking his head up and down a couple of times, looking at the house across the street, then back at the fire.

The rain was nice. It kept us from stressing about burning up the whole area.

"Can you cover us in this rain?" I asked Ned, who smiled and went back inside. We never understood why the Marines needed A-10's when they could train soldiers like Ned. Of course bigger problems need bigger stuff.

Webb got his tractor going and me and Beans stepped up onto his blade and shagged a ride. Back across the way, where a forest once stood, he lowered the blade and we got off. Webb grated out the tank tracks and filling in holes from uprooted trees.

If an enemy wanted to ambush us from there again, they were going to have to dig their own holes.

Me and Beans stepped to the fire to stay warm and dry out. Flames now hit fifty feet and we were forced back. It was nice to have a good fire going. A cleansing fire.

Webb, atop his tractor, bladed away. He rounded and topped off dozens potential fox holes. Then he hydrauliced his blade across and reeled a few stray trees that slipped the noose.

Me and Beans had nothing much to do except avoid getting cooked by the fire. We just stayed warm and wet.

Beans came alive with heat and humidity and kept throwing branches on the fire. "We had us some good fires in the Pacific," he said. "Entire islands!"

All was but done when that Red kid's truck entered the field and started circling, tire slinging mud at us.

Webb kept moving and stayed in the saddle.

But on their second turn, the boys nearly knocked me and Beans into the fire. I saw their eyes. I think they were trying to, but Red didn't want to get his truck too close. His nylon rebel rag melted to the flagpole on the last turn.

Then the truck got more sluggish as it turned to come at us again.

I smiled, seeing it's front tires were flat.

Beans holstered his automatic, seeing the magic behind Ned's plan.

The kid driver thought he was stuck in the mud and kept riding the gas as the rear tires deflated. I saw flash from the upper window of the VFW and knew Ned was carving his mark.

Now flat, the wheels just stopped as their beads broke free allowing the metal hubs to spin harmlessly in the mud to the tune of the revving engine.

I saw three boys in the front seat start arguing.

Then they jumped out, burying their shoes in the mud. Cursing they looked around and one picked up a mud clot and weighed it in his hand.

Webb low-idled the tractor engine and brought her to a stop between the youngsters and me and Beans. Webb stayed wary of Ned's fire line.

But I think he should have been more nervous about Beans, whose fingers were tapping the leather, sizing up the moment.

Maybe Beans was right. After all, a person never really knows what a sharp shooter was going to do in any given battle.

I walked over to Beans. I knew if he drew it wasn't for dancing. If he pulled his hog leg, someone was going to die.

The dirt clod came my way and the truck's passenger window exploded and fell onto the front seat.

We didn't hear the window bust out, because the fire roar.

But the boys did. They turned to the truck and took a few steps for it. They all wanted to jump back inside, but then the mirror sparked and the back window morphed as the safety glass fragmented. They turned to us and I thought they were going to charge.

So did Ned. That why he put some bullets into the mud at their feet, backing the gang away from Webb.

"You boys are in a gunfight!" Webb yelled over the tractor and fire roar.

The back window now fell out of the truck.

Red's main windshield popped as two bullet hole came a few feet apart. Then several more came underneath, making a smile. Then that window caved in.

All was quiet but for the sound of rain and updrafting fire that hissed and popped the wetness from the logs and evaporated the rain from the sky before it even hit the ground.

Then two, four and a half dozen holes plinked through the metal of the gas tank, driving the boys behind the truck.

Red, being the last, was hobbling something fierce and I knew Ned did more than dust him. Splinter charged into the open and grabbed Red and lugged him back behind his sinking truck, cursing. Then the truck gas tank caught fire. Holed, it was near drained and the ground around the area whooshed.

The boys took their tails and sprinted away.

Me and Beans nodded to each other as we took up a cable from Webb's tractor box and looped her through the brush guard of the truck and brought the hook back to the tractor.

I looked at Beans. Soaked and cold, he was younger. War made him young I swear it.

We saw Webb sitting high on his tractor, taking it all in.

He pushed the gears.

Then it happened. Fire climbed up from the ground, grabbing at the truck from under both sides of the bed and working it way to the engine.

The three slowed to a hard run across the muck away from us. They were nearly back to their driveway when they stopped. The fat one was having a hard go of it.

Beans tapped my arm and pointed at the kid lagging behind and smiled.

I didn't get what was funny, but you never know with Beans. What got him laughing could usually get someone arrested.

I stepped in front of Webb and waved him towards the fire.

"Let's light the fire!" Webb yelled.

Beans gave the thumbs up.

Webb revved the tractor.

I looked over at the boys who were now standing still in the field. Behind me their truck started to get dragged.

Webb's big tires dug hard and kept moving ahead. The long cable went taunt, as Webb arched around the fire on the upwind side so as not to boil his fuel. The cable cut through the fire as Webb dragged away. The fire burned at the taunt cable connecting Webb's tractor to Red's truck like a tug of war happening over hell.

The tractor won.

Gracefully the truck came to the fire, rolled into it and started climbing the fifty odd logs until it reached the summit, stopped, and stayed perched in the mountain of flame.

It made quite a sight, but nothing compared to the three stooges standing a hundred yards across the field in the rain. Poor little tykes had lost their Tonka.

Bean's took one of the two hooks attached to Webb's tractor hitch, pulled the pin on it and let the cable fall. Dropping the hook in the box on the tractor, he stepped back and Webb tractored on.

Me and Beans watched Webb's thick wire zip along the burning truck axel and come free of the inferno.

Liquid fire now poured from the doors as the plastic and rubber of the interior gave way.

Once the cable was clear, Webb stepped down and held out his hands to the heat. So close was he that his wet clothes were steaming. Dry spots appeared on his shirt as we stayed for a few minutes.

We shared some words but mostly thought back to the times where we used fire to sterilize towns and cities. Warmed, we stepped on Webb's plow and went back to our VFW, cable withering along in the mud behind us like a snake being dragged by the tail.

Once we had the gate locked behind us, we parked and helped Webb with the cable. It was still warm and covered in pine soot.

Then we went inside. Webb pulled out some beers, which was saying something because he was a tea-totting Baptist.

Ned appeared, coming down from his perch. The smell of gunpowder was on him like cologne.

"Nice shooting," Webb said.

"It's about time I'm appreciated!" Ned said.

We were all at the window watching the inferno blaze sixty feet into the sky. The truck was all but gone as the flamed roared around it. A small explosion puffed into the air.

"Didn't see that coming," Ned said.

"That's what got me nervous," I said.

"What?"

"The stuff we don't see coming."

"There will be hell to pay for what we done to that truck," Ned said.

"Think we'll get another ticket for burning without a permit?" Webb asked

"It's worth it," Beans said. "Hell for a day keeps the jitters away."

21

AFTER THE FIRE

Red blinked about eight times straight, gazing at the fire from behind Cell's basement window. Then his heart hurt bad and made his eyes sting. His fingers dug into his eyes to gouge out stress.

Then he exhaled, clawed the zit of the week on his back and turned to Pal and Splinter. "I got laid in that truck before I even had my license," he said.

Splinter stopped stroking his gauze wrap.

"Right in my dad's garage. I didn't even have my license," Red said.

"Who?" Cell asked, taking a hand from his stomach to knock mud from his pants.

"She was sweeter than Daisy Duke!" his voice went softer as if the steel fence beyond the roadway was a prison wall keeping him from freedom.

"I wouldn't stay by the window now that we have a light on," Splinter said, but Red was beyond reason.

"Who cares anymore," Red winced as he moved his leg and closed curtain to the bitter world. He couldn't be consoled by the non truck owners around him.

"What are we gonna do?" Cell asked.

"I'm gonna get them for this even if it kills me," Red said.

"One of those guys can shoot." Splinter said.

Cell pulled his hand back from his guts and looked at it for the first time. A deep burn had been laid across his knuckles. It now stung like an acid burn at the base of his pinky where a chunk of flesh was missing.

Splinter looked at Cell's hand and then held up his good hand and called the other two over. "Look at this!"

Splinter said. He to had a gash too. It was between his second and third knuckle on his remaining pinky. It was bleeding good because he flexed the finger below his heart and got the blood going.

"Rope burns," Cell said. "How'd we get them?"

Splinter looked at Red. Red nodded.

"It's not rope, stupid," Splinter said. "They're bullet burns. The sniper was trying to take off our pinkies!"

"Why's he want pinkies?" Cell asked.

Cell and Red looked at each other then at Splinter, who was looking at his feet. They went back to the window and looked south at the fire. The bulk of the timbers were just taking hold and heat waves danced in the rain and smoke. Black smoke billowed forth.

"He's not just going for our fingers," Red said.

"That's cause you still got yours!" Splinter said. "Wait! Did you…"

"Whatta ya mean?" Cell asked. He looked at Red who now sat on a crushed couch. It released a cloud of dust and Red took hold of his boot and grunted.

Red's pant let was soaked and it wasn't mud. The boot made a squishing sound as it slipped off his foot and thumped on the floor.

Splinter and Cell came over to Red.

It looked serious.

Red rolled up the pant leg and pulled down his sock, exposing skin covered in hair and blood.

Splinter took a knee and leaned in. "The bulled came out here," Splinter said, pointing to the back of the calf. "It's a lot bigger hole. I think you need to see a doctor for this?"

"So they can file a police report cause it's a gunshot?" Cell said.

Red turned to see out Cell's window. His truck sank deeper into the flames.

"I'm going to get them for this!" Red said. "They are going to pay!"

"The ones who burned your truck or the one who who shot you?" Splinter asked.

Cell came over, unscrewing a tube of Neosporin. "Berta gave us this and said to use it next time."

"Next time?" Splinter asked.

"She knew," Red said.

"She said to drown the wound in the goo," Cell said. "Said that it would do the trick."

"It's that simple?" Splinter said.

"What's his face in history said Noesporin would have saved a half million Civil War soldiers," Cell said and he injected a good squirt of the medicine into Red's bullet holes and wrapped a clean white sock around the calf. "Remember, Berta said a little blood flow is a good thing."

"Looks like their getting a taste of their own!" Red said, pointing out the window. "Coppers!"

Splinter and Cell jumped to the window. "Fire Department too!" Splinter said.

"We won!" Cell claimed and stood up, arms high in victory, then he recoiled sharply as his rib stabbed him with venom.

"They didn't call the cops." Splinter said. "Having the cops come ain't calling them."

"Might be," Cell held.

"Sit down," Red said, losing his truck enable him to see the big picture. "The conquered squad is the one who rats the other out. Splint's right. Get up and kill the lights. I don't want Deep Pockets around here."

"How you gonna claim insurance on the truck if you can't call the cops?" Cell asked.

"I only have PO and PD," Red said.

"I think we should hide," Splinter said. "They'll be coming for us."

Police Chief Tabbs trumped his officers and kicked them out of the V.F.W. where they were making the veterans more hardheaded. He then sat at the table in Wendell's chair and looked at Lefty and Ned.

Webb and Beans kept playing cards, working on their poker faces as the Brass fired questions.

"This Wendell's chair?" Chief asked.

"I'll take two," Beans dropped two cards and Ned dealt him two more.

"How'd you get by our fence?" I asked and looked outside. I saw Brance was there from the hardware. I knew he had the combination.

"Brance from the hardware," Chief said. "He came to me a few days ago and now I pulled him in on it."

"Why didn't you just knock and hit the buzzer?" I asked. "What are we? Something to be afraid of?" I lowered my cards as if the Chief was trying to scope them out. I didn't trust the man.

"Something like that," Chief said. "I'm still trying to figure it out. "Bringing guns into public places. Riding tanks on the road. Starting fires. And what's the truck frame doing in the fire!"

"It's been buried in that forest for years. You should thank us for cleaning up the place!" Webb said. "And I have a triangle on the back of my Sherman. Used her for some agriculture. Kind of like an industrial mower, that's all."

"Who called it in?" I asked. We could talk normal now that the fire truck sirens were winding down.

"You can see it for miles," Chief said. "You called us in."

"We ain't talking 'till we know," I said.

Chief looked around at a few of his officers who had loitered back in to get out of the rain. One had opened our fridge as if it were a public kitchen. A good chunk of the Fire Department force seemed to be in our V.F.W. too, and it wasn't even Pig Roast Primetime.

The Fire Marshal seemed upset but Chief kept nodding him quiet. He got the officers and some to his crew out of the kitchen. We had our space back.

It was good to see so many stepping outside back in the rain and mud.

"Old Lady Timmons. It's on tape." Chief said.

"It is?"

"It is. And its disturbing."

"We had permission," Webb said. "Those trees had to go. Ain't no big deal. I told him I could do it with the tank and that it'd be no problem."

"Who?" Chief asked.

"The landowner," Webb said.

"Who's that?"

"Find out yourself."

"Maybe I will. Why?"

"You don't like how we did it?"

"I don't like any of this! I don't like tanks grinding up my streets, crushing down forest, tearing up asphalt. Scaring old ladies. I don't like it at all. And I don't like Brance's theory either!"

"Who's Brance?" Beans asked, looking up from his cards for the first time.

"He's from the hardware store. Says you've been having trouble with some boys. Teenagers. Those ones at the funeral. And one of them is missing. Been missing for four days! And who are you?" Chief's face was going a shade of purple.

"You don't have to worry about getting to know me," Beans said. "I don't make friends with people like you."

"One of the three kids at the funeral is missing?" I asked.

"Maybe Brance should stick to hardware and leave the wetware to someone else," Ned said.

"You know what I'm talking about. There should be four of them!" Chief said.

"What's your point?" Webb asked. "Is he a taxpayer?"

"Don't push me, Webster, Deacon Board or not!" Chief said. "You want to push and I'll push all of you into a full blown investigation."

"What are you investigating?" I asked.

"You should make it official, then you could bill us for it." Webb asked. "A lot of corporate hours out there standing in the rain."

Chief looked at us and held up his fingers. "First the flag. The fence and gate. Then the tanks. One of my officers said he chased off some kids who filled one with water. And now we got a missing kid. And I don't like you having weapons at a funeral! Or leaning against the walls!" he pointed at the two Thompsons. And why are you wearing the .45s? Expecting a war? Those boys hassling you? Is Brance right? You can talk to me. There's no shame. What's going on?"

We just looked at our cards, then at each others faces. Then at Webb's.

"It was Lefty's idea," Webb said.

"It better be good," Chief said. "And you better remember Lefty, I'll clamp irons on you one handed or no!"

"She's a gaser, Chief." I said.

"A what?"

"He's a diesel man," Ned said.

"And I'm The Chief! I don't buy it!" The soldiers looked at each other and Chief realized he wasn't getting anywhere.

"I'm about ready to drag you downtown. Put you in a box. Wreck your day."

I looked at Beans. If he spoke it would go south. Webb, well he couldn't lie to save the church offering. Ned was to methodical to connect all the dots so I put my cards down, face up. It was a full house. Good enough to get me some gold teeth if we were only ourselves.

They were all looking at me anyways.

"Used to be a lot of things could wreck our day, Chief, but lately it's the nothing. Doing nothing. It's the nothing that wrecks our day," I said.

"But we don't need to get threats for making improvements to our V.F.W. For making displays so the public can come and see our sacrifices!" I said. I was on a role, careful not to lay it on too thick.

Chief looked at me."So you tote around all these weapons, burn down a small forest and an old truck to boot all for your display? And you expect me to swallow it?"

"You can't have a WWII display on a nice grassy knoll!" I said. "It was a war of fire and crushed metal. That's what we're building, Chief! We're building a life-size diorama of burned out buildings, vehicles and infantry tanks. A person shouldn't have to go to our nations capitol to see our sacrifices! And you can tell Knoxel and Brance down at the hardware that we appreciate their helping us with the fence. But we need to keep the project a secret until we can secure all the necessary equipment safely, and get all the right permits."

Chief rubbed his chin.

"Tell Brance to get his facts strait. You were at the funeral. You saw Wendell's impact on those children!" As I said this I looked at my friends. I knew I said too much. Now we were going to have to build a life size diorama. Assuming Chief bought the passel of stretchers I just fed him.

"You need to communicate better with what you're doing from now on. And as for the fire, I'll talk the Marshal to make sure you only get the minimum fine for burning without a permit."

We all knew what that meant. Webb would have another trophy to toast too.

"You should propose your project to the Town Counsel if you intend to charge money." He gave us some contacts. "Maybe the Pocketville Chamber can cross-promote your exhibit during another public event to attract more visitors. That's how it works. No more secrets. Understand?"

All four of us nodded as if we agreed not to urinate in public anymore.

Standing up he made way to the door. "I think it's a good idea," he said. "It'll bring some attention and allow you to put your hobbies to good use." He put on his hat. "But you got to let us know what your doing before you do it." Having said that, he left.

All was quiet.

"No one can be that stupid," Beans said.

Ned collected cards and re-dealt. "You sure Brance told him about our war?" he asked.

I looked around. "I picked up some hinters from the Chief but that was all," I said. "Chief already said this and that. I just mixed up what he said with what he wanted to hear."

Since our fire was about one third the temperature of the Hiroshima Hell Storm, the Fire Department decided to let it burn itself out. It took three days, so they had to issue us the minimum ticket each day of the blaze to cover their cost of coming and going.

It was worth it.

We threw on the rest of the logs. And for the next few days, things seemed to die down.

When it cooled, we dragged the truck frame onto our property and sat it under the flag by our tanks like a trophy. Its engine had been cooked black in pine carbon

Looking back, we should've dragged the truck frame over here. We should not have put a spot light on it at night. We should've rubbed the noses of those kids in it.

It happened during our card game on a Tuesday night.

22

TANK ATTACK AND COUNTERATTACK

The idea came from Pal and they should have known better, since the three of them were all behind on their visitations and food deliveries. But from behind his oil grimed eyes, he was glad they had come. It was the first time he had seen them together since Splinter had gotten a finger shot off.

They were a nervous bunch, each wearing their insults wrapped in bandages and gauze. Red limped terrible and his back was starting to hurt from walking crooked.

"And I still haven't crapped," Cell said.

One hand of Splinter was wrapped up and the other oozed puss from an infection.

They were men without leadership, soldiers without a mission, and mercenaries without a paycheck.

"I don't like being here with them here," Splinter said, nodding to the line of pick-up trucks on the other side of the parking lot near the ramp to the VFW.

"Shut up!" Red said. "They're just sitting inside playing cards."

"Then let's get it done!" Pal told his team the news. "I'm telling you the working tank is unlocked," he repeated.

"So," Cell said. "We still don't have the keys, Pal. A lot of good it'll do us with no keys."

"Don't tell me you ran off and left stupid on me! It's a tank. You don't need keys. You think they had time to make a million sets of keys for a million tanks in the middle of a World War? Don't be dumb! And why would you need a key if they were always manned by guys with guns?" Pal was yelling a bit because he couldn't hear himself that well.

"How?" Splinter asked.

"You find the fire button. This one still has one in it. Climb into the other one and I'll show you."

Pal was feeling good. His friends had given him some outdated drops that Berta had left over clinic to help his ears. The medicine was for horses but he didn't care. Now his left was receiving about fifty-fifty and the blown one was getting less sore as the medicine ate away at the caked blood.

"I don't trust it," Red said, looking up at the tank. It was night but big halogens had replaced the buzzing pole light. They were in the open but no one cared. Who was going to complain? The ones that were filling them with holes?

"I thought about that," Pal said. "It could be a trap no doubt. So get a chain on the lid so it can't close. Then it's fool proof!"

"What's foolproof?" Splinter asked.

"Tankjacking the tank, stupid!" Pal yelled an octave high.

Splinter and Red walked to the tank, but Cell took a step back at the news and looked across the street.

"My mom hates that thing pointing at her. Slaps at me. Like it's my fault," he said

"You sure we can get it working?" Splinter asked.

"I can do it!" Red said. He was looking at his truck frame now. Smelling it too. It's not right what they did to my truck. You don't mess with a man's first truck. "Gimme the basics on what you know," Red asked Pal.

Pal did. He told him the start and kill switches and the two tube-like mounts that controlled the tank tracks.

"Push forward if you want to go forward. Pull back if you want to go back. It's like mowing a lawn with an eXMark™. I'm telling you we can do this! Mine still has all this crap in it and I read the operators manual!"

"When?"

"What are you talking about? You forget I've been in here forever? What else am I to do?"

"What are we gonna do once it's running?" Cell asked. He didn't see the light.

"What do you think?" Pal said. "You don't move around too good. You better stay here with me. But they're going to ruin the VFW! Run it down. Crush this little compound! No more third Sunday roast beef fundraisers for Pocketville Boy Scouts! We owe them that, Cell. Look at what they're doing to us!"

"I used to have a chain in my truck bed," Red said.

"Crack to it, Cell!" Pal barked.

Cell came back with a carbon black chain, hands and shirt layered in soot.

Splinter and Red hooked the chain to the hatch, pulled it through an eye in the back the hooked the chain to itself with the other end. The chain moved quiet on the tank. Inches of solid steel muffled the sound.

"Won't close now!" Splinter said.

"Splinter, you go and climb inside. Fumble around awhile," Red said. "See if any other wires need to be tripped." Red stepped back and watched Splinter climb up and in to check for booby traps. He wished he had more men like Splinter under his command.

Across the way, Pal could only see Cell. Pal scratched his bloody scalp with long fingernails, lined black with oil sludge. "Are they inside, Cell?"

"Splinter is," Cell said.

Splinter came back topside. "We can do this Red! And I even found a light switch It's broke. It only shines red, but you can still see!"

Red climbed and entered the tank, then he sat in the command and control. It was like Pal said. An ON switch. An OFF one. And some metal leg things coming up from the floor to steer her by. I can do this! he said to himself. He called Pal's phone. "I can do this!" he yelled.

"Now your talking!" Pal replied. "Cap'n Crunch Time!"

Splinter came topside and gave Cell the thumbs up.

Cell stepped well to one side then retreated to the prisoner visitation area.

Pal smiled inside his black confine. He heard the engine fire then die. Then it fired again and stayed on. Pal sloshed through the slim water and went to the fresh air slide and peered out.

Cell was in view. He was backing up, not like his position in case Red actually got the thing going. Good old Red, he thought. You can't replace common sense of a redneck!

Pal saw Cell jump to the left and stop in front of him.

The ground shook.

The tank engine had engaged the treads. The tracks were churning forward.

In the bowels of the dead tank, Pal smiled. His unbrushed teeth, a testament to his sentence.

In the guts of the running tank, Red straightened back, loosened his neck and looked out his slide. He had a pretty good view. Splinter stayed up top to get the fresh air and full panoramic perspective of driving in a machine designed to crush everything around it.

"Engine sounds good," Red said into the phone. "Real good!"

Inside the building that Tuesday night, Beans threw another four gold teeth into the pot on a bluff.

I called and he lost.

Ned took up the cards to deal and I sensed Beans had bigger beef in his boiler.

Neither him or Webb were focused. They were handing over chompers and bragging rights. I had been making a killing for two nights. I looked at them. Beans and Webb are working on some other scheme. They're playing another game. A mission. I saw this as true.

I looked at Ned. We didn't care what those two did. We were like the Pollocks and Hollanders getting rich in the 1930's because those peaceful Germans were paying top dollar for metal and technology.

So we wised up and stopped being greedy. Now we were curious. Last night we asked them what they had been doing out under the flag by the Shermans.

"Misinformation is the key to winning any war," Webb had said, as if me and Ned had become turnip truck drivers.

Beans had stayed quiet. But whatever it was, the sting in my Everas hand now said Beans idea-ed it. That got me nervous. Beans wasn't right in the head in a way that was very wrong. He was a man to be in charge only if something needed to be conquered.

Teeth on the table rattled and we looked around to see who was shaking.

"I don't believe it," Ned jumped up from the table.

The rest of up fumbled our way to the security monitor to watch.

Webb took up a Thompson submachine gun that had been propped in the corner and disappeared into the back to check the flank with Ned. He seemed ready to go. He wasn't surprised.

Beans either.

Only me and Ned seemed to have our pants down.

Ned came back. Flustered, he didn't know what to do. He circled.

I think he was looking for a hole in the ground. Good old holes. He wanted to gopher.

"Relax," Beans told him.

"How did you know?" I asked, watching the tank creep forward on the TV monitor. I pulled my .45 nonetheless. It wouldn't do much good, but when tanks rumble up the big stuff from in the ground, you grab iron on instinct!

"Look at the tank," Beans said, pointing.

"You know something we don't?" Ned turned to Beans.

He gave us a dumb innocent look and turned away, but I knew better.

I tilted my head but Ned was looking out the front door.

The engine was turning over inside the Sherman on high idle and then the tires started screeching against metal.

Ned was thinking now. He was planning retreat. He looked at me and nodded.

I didn't care what plan Beans and Webb had worked up. My carcass was going with Ned. No one goes against a Sherman with a pea-shooter.

Webb came out and joined us. "Isn't that a beautiful sound?" he said, putting his arms across mine and Ned's shoulders.

I knew enough about armor that I was thinking like Ned. I was thinking tuck tail.

But Beans and Webb weren't. And there was something wrong with how relaxed they were.

A shaking hand came up to Webb's chin and wiped saliva from the right side of his mouth. It wasn't shaking with fear. It was adrenaline slime.

I looked at Beans who was being entertained.

Beans caught my eyes then nodded me back to the tank. It had crossed half our yard, plowing our flagpole as if it were a toothpick.

I checked behind me, making sure the path was clear. The safety on my .45 clicked off and I racked a shell by pinching the barrel between my knees. If a person got between me and my escape, I was now prepared to blow him in two pieces

Pal and Cell weren't stupid. Between pneumonia and broken guts, they were wising up to their place in the universe. They were thankful for their shelter in and around the broken tank as Red and Splinter shook the ground, powering the good tank across the driveway.

Cell moved towards Pal's talk zone at the tank slide. "When is he going to turn?" he asked Pal.

Pal didn't hear him.

Inside the command seat of the Sherman, Red jacked the steering arms as he rumbled along at two miles an hour. He called Splinter to him after he squished the flagpole. "I gotta get me one of these!" his smile moved his ears.

"You gotta turn?" Splinter pointed left towards the VFW from above.

Red pulled on the left steering arm and pushed on the right one. "I see you!" he nodded at the three men in the doorway of the VFW. "Better run and hide!"

The men didn't move.

Red leaned forward to the armored viewing slide to see them better as his tank rolled onward.

"Why aren't you turning?" Splinter asked.

"Just gimme a second," Red pulled and pushed harder on the steering, straining to turn left or right. "Now I got it!"

Pal raised his phone and dialed.

The right track snagged the halyard on the crumpled flagpole and hoisted the Stars and Strips from the mud and sucked it up and under the track and shredded it.

"Answer the phone!" Red yelled.

"Hello?" Splinter asked.

"You gotta turn. Use the arms!" Pal yelled. He saw an old man point to the main gate which was guarding the compound.

Splinter looked at Red who was jamming on the turning arms. "Pal said you gotta turn!"

"I'm trying to turn, you moron! It's not responding!"

They both looked ahead and saw the gate and watched their cannon punch a hole through the fence, which then buckled under the power of the tank and wrapped around the turret, scrapping off paint as each cement fence pole got ripped out of the ground and started following. Then the link fence started stretching.

Across the street, a very large woman in front of her TV looked over at her glass of Diet Pepsi. For a moment the ice seemed to vibrate, then the top cube jumped down and nestled with the others. The lady frowned. Maybe I should buy that small refrigerator from WalMart™ and keep it by my chair I could use another footrest. She then moved her swollen toes. One was going black again from a lack of insulin. She wanted to massage it but it was too far away.

Across her front yard, inside a devouring tank, Red looked at Splinter and let the steering arms go. "It doesn't want to turn for some reason." Red dared look out the forward slot and saw Cell's house getting bigger. "We got us some trouble! Let's get out of here!" He jumped from the command seat then bumped into Splinter's backsides. "Get going!"

Splinter was stopped cold in the belly of the beast. Above him at the escape hatch, a thick band of crushed, twisted, withering chain link fence, had constricted around the entire turret and the open hatch and had driven him below. He reached for it and something snapped as if it were a snake recoiling after a strike. Some barb wire which used to be atop that gate was still attached to the ground to the right. It slithered across the hatch, nipping out bites from whatever it touched.

Behind the tank, at the compound, Beans stepped out onto a small porch at the VFW. He had just poured himself a fresh cup of coffee. Raising it to his lips, he took a sip.

"What going on?" I asked Webb. "What did you two do?"

"It looks like they did it!" Webb said.

"We've must of left the tank unlocked!" Beans said and we watched the tank drag hundreds of feet fence as it chewed its way across the street and closed in on the TV House.

"Good thing I disconnected the steering so it couldn't do some serious damage." Webb said. "Safety first."

"Wendell would have like this," Beans said.

"Battles and witches," Ned said.

We listened to the tank caterpillar towards the house emitting its normal, twisted metal hissing sound.

"They better shut her down before it eats the house," I said. "Webb? Tell me they can it shut it down. Or did you monkey with the kill switch too?"

"You know diesels," Webb said, taking a few steps forward. "It only takes a loose wire to make them run until they're out of fuel!"

Back in the VFW parking lot, Cell stood up and walked into the light. "My house!" he said. He took a step into the open. "Mom!"

Red dove back to the control seat, phone to his ear.

"Kill it! Kill it!" Pal was yelling. "The Red Switch! Upper right! Hurry!"

Red saw the switch. "Gotcha!" He turned it.

The switch came off the wall and fell to the vibrating floor.

"Oops," Red said and looked out the view slide. "Get us out of here!"

"We're fenced in!" Splinter cursed back.

The tank then breached the yard. It folded a ghetto bush. Then it punched through Cell's front door and went kilter ten degrees as it crushed the hollow concrete front steps. It smashed through outer wall and crushed through the main floor and dove, gun first into the basement.

Splinter fell down. Stuff poured into the hatch, through the barb and tearing chain mesh.

The treads were soon chewing against concrete of the far wall something awful. But because of posi-traction, the right took hold and climbed some of the far wall, turning the tank left. From there it commenced to cut through the water, sewer and electrical lines, showing the basement in sparks. But still it consumed, cracking through its first load bearing support wall, caving in some of the roof and severing a gas line.

The fat woman found herself in her basement. Screaming, she saw herself unprepared for a world of diesel exhaust, shaking floors, spraying water and snapping sparks. Covered in pink insulation and dusty sheet rock walling, she managed to stand. She looked at her feet and the ground where everything small was vibrating. Her house was breathing! Water was over her ankles.

She then lifted her head. Her house had become a bowl of cereal and she blinked and realized from the open barrel of the Sherman Tank that a reality was upon her that she was not prepared for. She screamed. Then, with a quickness that amazed even her, she leaped out of the way into a clearing under a section of uncollapsed main floor. She watched the track of the beast grind by her.

From above, on the sloping main floor, the TV slide into the basement, dislocated her shoulder and rolled under the crushing tank tread.

The lady blinked hard, looking for the stairs.

Cell ran onto his front lawn as the roof fell in.

A gas explosion sent a fireball upward, igniting all the small pieces of the house as it puked them into the sky in a big orange and black cloud. Burning insulation, shingles and wood fragments rained down on Cell, who had been knocked on his back. In the firelight, the situation looked worse.

"Wow!" Beans said from across the street, taking another sip. "You can't take the monkey out of the mishap."

Most of us had a hand up, instinctively shielding our faces from the blast wave.

Beans didn't. He seemed to welcome it like one would an ocean breeze.

Webb looked right and left and nodded. No surprise so far. Battles and witches! The thing had been pointed right at the house! Maybe they should have thought about that.

Cell was back on his feet. Forgetting his fear of going into the open, and overcoming the pain in his stomach. He now became a rescuer. "Mom!"

Before him the screams of the woman rose from the quagmire.

"I wonder it he wants to hit her again?" Ned asked.

"Was that a real scream or just one of the old ones?" I asked.

"We're back in Real Time," Ned said.

In the basement, the big momma was back on her feet. Disheveled scalp under singed off hair, dress scorched down to her bra, and blooddust dirt across her bare arms and legs, she eyed her green elephant.

It was her against it all over again. Story of her life. "Get out of my house!" she yelled but knew he was like the others and beyond reason. She looked to escape and swam over debris for the steps. Reaching the twisted stair, she neared a hanging wire as her foot stepped in the water.

The wire reached out and touched her arm and for a moment she tried to smack it loose with a backhand. She wanted to move her other arm but it was frozen. She then smelled smoke and looked at the flab getting sizzled off her arm as if a mad scientist was giving her Lipo Suction. Why doesn't it hurt? She stared at her electric leech.

"Mom!" A hand reached down to her but it was too far away.

Pieces of planking, glass, a cast iron bathtub and half a porcelain toilet fell as the bathroom above gave way.

She looked up at her son. She reached for him but her body was now shaking as the wire that once fed the breaker box burrowed thirstily into her arm. She heard her boy screaming. Her ears worked just fine. So did her eyes. She watched the starry eye of the green monster pass by.

Then the eye seemed to blink as the tank pivoted on the cast iron bathtub, catch grip and explode it into fragments.

She saw her son just above her.

The jolly green green machine now rumbled straight at her.

Finally. She thought.

The right tread pinched down on her ankle as the left tread tore the wire from her arm.

She could now scream and scream she did as the right tank track climbed from her foot to her knee.

Inside the tank, Red opened his dust burning eyes for a second and stole a look through the view slid. He saw Cell's mom, whose dress and entire outer layer of skin had been burned off her body, get slammed on her back by the advancing machine. He knew he was going over her.

She watched her leg go under. Her attack came so slow, so different from the wife-beaters she always seemed to marry. But this one didn't really hurt that bad either. She saw her leg muscle get herniated through her fascia and appear on both sides as the track climbed to her hip, searching for traction. She didn't scream, she just looked up to her boy and reached out her hand to him. There he is! Trying to save me! He's such a good boy!

Cell tried to turn away but couldn't. His outstretched arm held him to her and he saw the tank grind over his mother, searching for traction and finding none on the slippery surface of blood, sinew, intestine, bone and good-ole white fat.

23

Runaway Tank

Mr. Sherman tanked the teenagers on a course laid out by least resistance. Searching for a way out of Cell's basement, it ground up death into paste. Like an insect breaking from a cocoon, it chewed what used to have purpose into dust.

Every time a track bit into the concrete basement wall, it turned the machine back into the hole and repacked all it touched to debris and slush as water poured in.

Then its two front runners hit the back concrete wall at the same time, took hold and climbed. The beast broke out the far side of Cell's house, dragging flaming timbers, wires and part of the framed roof as well as a good wad of the VFW security fencing.

Across the street, Webb stood ahead of the rest and turned back. "And those fools on Capital Hill said Sherman's are bad tanks!"

The tank crossed the back yard, tipping over trees as it crawled for the woods like a smoldering dragon.

Inside, its passengers dared again to peek out the slide. Smoke filled their area and some concrete, stud frames and sheetrock were seeping atop the hatch.

Red and Pal had long since exhausted their original profanities and were now repeating engrained combo's.

"We gotta get outta here!" Red abandoned the sabotaged control center and entered a new era of despair as he went to the hatch.

Splinter was braced in a corner, his hand bleeding with torn stitches from trying to de-clog the escape hatch. Now the tunnel freedom was slippery with blood. He had failed many times to exit.

As the Sherman Tank rolled on, its next fifteen minute performance would have granted itself another military contract as it left a damage path across a mile of northern Kent County.

After taking out a telephone pole and exploding a transformer in a thunderclap, it kept grinding east, trailing a tangle of sparks and electrical wires like a runaway dog with a dozen leashes.

Zapped and jolted, Red and Pal spent twenty minutes making escape attempts out the hatch, deeming the clutter of metal and wire, snared by the open hatch, more unsafe after every failure.

The tank then took its passengers downhill in a sudden lurch and the elevation dropped until the terrain went level. Perfectly level.

The boys looked at each other as all went smooth as if they were on the salt flats of Death Valley.

Red jumped to the slide, thinking they had stopped.

"What's up?" Splinter asked. "We stopped?"

"We're still moving, Splinter, but not for long!" Red jumped back to the hatch and attacked the clutter, veins growing under his skin like pencils.

"What?" Splinter said.

"Dig for you life. We're on McLarry's!"

Splinters face turned a shade of pink in the red cockpit light above the navigation table.

As the tank drove out onto eight inches of ice of McLarry's pond, an ominous crack reverberated as its left track collapsed through the ice. Then the tank plunged down through the ice sideways, dragging its debris field of into the water like tentacles of a giant squid. The small, red interior light flickered, as water poured into the hatch, but it stayed on.

Ice water stabbed Cell and Splinter to scream as the tank rested sideways in the mud of the pond bed ten feet below a gaping hole in ice.

Waist deep in no time, Red lunged forward and dragged the front view hatch closed, stemming the water.

In seconds all was quiet and still except the drone of the diesel driving the tracks and churning mud until water gagged the air intake, choking the engine. It suffocated and died and left the boys fighting to squeeze into a few feet of trapped air above bitter cold water.

All went still. Quiet. Calm. Peace.

"Where are we?" Splinter whispered.

"At the bottom of McLarry's Pond!" Red started cursing and the shakes came as the levels of hypothermia crisscrossed though his body.

The boys looked to main roof hatch, which was now under water at their waist. Above them was the right wall of the tank.

"We gotta get though that hatch!" Red said as if it was a nostril on the face of death.

Splinter nodded. "How?"

Red looked at him, death swirling around inside his eyes. "Squirm until you're almost dead and your body will freak out and go super human!"

"Now?" Splinter didn't like the plan.

"Now! The longer we wait, the weaker we get!"

A mile away, Old Lady Timmons stood at her front door holding the phone. What had happened ousted prime-time TV and her phone replaced the remote control as her tool of choice. It took a few minutes to convince the 911 operator that another police emergency had happened in as many weeks.

"The Army is coming!" she repeated with the same passion as Paul Revere. "They drove through my neighborhood in tanks!"

"Please start from the beginning and tell me that again." the 911 lady said.

"No. You've heard it twice! I don't say things three times to anybody except my poodle!"

Then the 911 switchboard started lighting up across the board and dispatch realized the north end of Pocketville had a situation.

Our VFW compound looked more like a militarized zone than ever with the fence torn and twisted like barbwire on a beachhead. Exhaust diesel and civilian smoke stained the air and stung our noses.

Shadows underfoot came from our floodlights, a streetlight and the headlamps of a few rubberneckers in cars were at the corner watching the blaze.

The four of us crossed the road. Shoulder to shoulder we walked, some better than others.

Webb kept stepping ahead us. "I say we buy this dump and add it to our display! How's that sound, Lefty?"

I said nothing, but I could still think, and that got me nervous as we closed in on the fat boy.

He had his back to us, looking into the pit that used to be his house.

We knew his tank-regurgitated mother was down below him. Electrical sparks still snapped and popped, removing the shadows around for a moment as small flashes of lightning erased darkness. Good thing. They kept igniting pockets of gas and keeping the explosions from getting too powerful.

We crossed the road, our footfalls quiet inside the snow-packed ruts of the tank tracks. We closed the distance and fanned out.

"He's dodged death before," Beans said. "Rotten German bullets."

We looked at him, wondering what he meant.

The teenager stood before us, shoulders slumped, looking down. Before him was the pit, covered in competing shadows from the street light and the VFW floods.

We stepped onto yard snow and crushed to ice. It crunched underfoot with no squeaks because the temps were up near freezing.

"It's the young that are the most dangerous," I said.

"That's when most of us got killed." Webb said. "Kid Krouts were crummy losers."

"Remember when they go, they don't like to do it alone. Only Japs seemed to do alone. After they killed off their families that is," Beans said.

"Of course," Webb said.

"Don't fight him," Ned said. "Just kill him."

"What if his mother's still alive?" I asked. I'd seen miracles before. But I knew I was overly optimistic. Not getting devoured by tank in a tight debris field took more than divine intervention.

By now we were right behind the boy and stopped, thinking he had become deaf and dumb because the horror.

"Shell shock," Webb said.

He was right.

We waited. No rush to do anything now. We looked down below and saw what was left of the woman. We didn't turn away, but took it all in. We'd squeeze the disturbing scene somewhere in our minds. Human memory can store more horror than most people know.

"That's my mom," Cell said to us, still facing the squish that was a parent. He seemed to stomach it well enough.

"Yes," Beans said.

"But she didn't have anything to do with this."

"So." Beans said.

Cell turned his wide body and squared his shoulders. Behind him was the hole. In front was us. He was cornered.

Ned turned from the hole and nodded for me to look into it.

I did. I saw it.

"What are you going to do to me, Cap'n? You gonna be the tough soldier again? You think you can knock me off the stage with a dead man's arm?" Cell asked Ned, chin down and eyes up, peering at us underneath low hanging eyebrows. He was going to charge.

He lunged at Ned.

Expected.

Beans lowered himself and shielded Ned, using his rawboned body to stand the boy up.

I saw Webb raising his Thompson and shook my head. You can't just kill someone in Pocketville. Plus Beans was in the Kill Zone.

The Thompson still rose.

I stepped between Webb and the boy and rapped the kid's skull with my .45. He went down hard as I stared Webb's Thompson barrel back to the earth.

Ned and Beans dropped to their knees. "There," Ned pointed. He and Bean's pushed.

Me and Webb each put a foot to the effort and together we rolled the body over the edge and into the hole made by Webb's tank.

The boy landed on the live wire and it fed juice into his carcass. If he needed to jump start his heart, it might have done the trick. Instead, it just electrocuted him.

It took a minute or so before we knew he was a dead. It never comes quick. We watched that too.

"It's like the Electric Chair?" Beans said and he and Ned stood and brushed snow from their knees. "Too humane for my taste."

"Hmm," Ned grunted.

"It's not too humane," Web said, watching smoke poured from the boy's chest.

An explosion down the road a bit brought our heads up.

Our floodlights and the streetlights went dead as the entire electric line failed.

"Transformer," Webb said.

"From grounding the kid?" Beans asked.

"The tank," Webb said. That made sense. No surprise there. It's what they do.

I wiped blood and hair from my pistol in the darkness with a piece of pink, smoking insulation.

Webb looked around. A few cars still had their lights beaming off in the direction of the tank, but all else was dark. He walked to the hole. "Why is it that some roosters don't have spurs?" Webb asked. "Well, hell! Battles and witches for Wendell!" He spit into the sparking chasm.

We stood there and looked at the dead.

"Let's go deal some cards," Ned said.

At this we looked around. I nodded. Cards sounded good.

"Better track down my tank first," Webb said. "It's what an innocent person would do," he rubbed his whiskers. "It's what a victim would do, right?"

Beans, Ned and I looked at him. We supposed he was right. But those men, the kind from our generation who always had general complaints had been gone for a long time.

"Dunno," Ned said. "The victims have died long ago. Give or take."

"Then I better go get my truck," I said. "Frost is still in the ground. We'll track her down and finish it."

24

Firefight

Life was filled with guns and war
And all of us got trampled on the floor
Children died the days grew cold
A piece of bread could buy a bag of gold
There's no time to change your mind
—D.C. Talk, Left Behind

Pal backed up until he bumped the steel wall of his prison. His voice had gone still. The inner one. Until a few moments ago, it had always whispered to him. The utterings we're never what he wanted to hear, but they came nevertheless.

Pal! Don't bust into that V.F.W.!
Think Pal! Don't pee on that recorder!
Yo, Dog! Don't torment Splinter's pet!
Pal! Don't paintball that old man!
Pal! Moron! Don't build another potato gun!
Hey! Don't shoot the V.F.W.!
Listen Pal! Don't aim a potato gun at a person!
Pal! Don't go inside that tank!
Shh! Don't cuss at them old men!
Hold still! Don't throw your turd at him!
Pal! It's too easy to carjack a tank! You better think it through!

Now, as Pal's hypothermed, weakened, infected, feverish body slumped against the cold, wet steel, he listened. He wanted to hear the whisper. The guidance. He tried to hear. He even closed his eyes, but there was only silence. The stillness. He heard the sound of silence. Not because the bombs blew his ears, but because his heart was dying.

He had always heard it was possible to wreck out his heart. That it could go bad. And now he knew it that way and he had no one to blame but himself. He listened to no one, and made up his the rules, so he didn't have to answer to the voice. And now his guilt had gone cold. The voice had gone away. Perhaps for good.

If a mirror was before him, light wouldn't be needed to see himself. Like the medieval creature that eats the living to feed dead innards, Pal knew his soul had lost its color.

He felt like a poached egg yoke in an unbreakable shell.

So when he saw the four men role Cell into the pit. And saw the streetlight flicker in a power drain, he knew they had killed him.

"What have I done?" he asked the silence. "What have I created? Who have I awoken?"

He felt another explosion in his bones and nerves. Whether it was far away or near he didn't care. He looked out and all was black but for narrow tubes of headlights far away.

He looked to the hatch again and the silhouettes of killers coming towards him. Going to the emergency bag, he opened it, reached inside then went back to the view slide.

Pal let them come. He drew and pointed the .22 revolver, counting their steps, getting the feel of their movements. Predicting their stride. His finger tightened. It was his turn now.

Webb looked behind us for a moment, not liking the complete darkness but for carlights of the rubbers down south on the roadside.

I went to squeeze my Everaus hand, disliking the sting.

"Your diesel's too heavy to go across country," Ned said.

We saw no movement in our parking lot as we crossed the line where the fence was. It was back to how we liked it. Before us sat our trucks. They reflected the flickers of light that sparked from the dying house. We kept our trucks clean, hating the winter salt from the snow plows. The prisoner tank was still and dark, absorbing light like a green hole. It seemed to officially be a coffin.

"Ground's still frozen," I said. "She'll do fine."

Carlights were behind us now, illuminating the crater. Sirens sounded off in the night, coming in from many different directions and muzzle flashes came at us from the slide under the 177 Sherman Tank cannon.

Ned snarled in pain. Beans yelled and I suppose me and Webb mouthed something too. But it all got drowned out by thunder as Ned, Beans and I stepped forward, drawing down, opening fire with our big bore .45's, and roaring off enough gumption to take the sperm out of a Kansas T-storm.

The tank lit up in spark as our lead bounced off. Ned and Beans stepped right, flanking towards the compound and kept a steady roll of hell-fire pouring forth. Beans ejected an empty clip and slammed another in place without breaking his roll of thunder.

I broke to the left and kept my weight into the handgun, bringing her back on line after it bucked upward on every shot.

No more fire came from the slide and I knew I missed more than the others. But I also knew I punched at least one round into the slide. One would likely be all that was needed.

Going left, I wasn't interested in getting a flank. I only wanted to get out of the way of Webb and his Thompson.

As the wicked whine of Webb's long, lead bullets whipped and ricocheted off the armored vehicle, I dropped into the mud, gun forward and emptied my clip.

We all knew we drove the ambusher into the bottom of the toilet funnel so we stopped shooting.

Gunfire echoed off in the darkness. Some getting tangled between our ears. Then the sirens came back.

Gunsmoke engulfed, then it oozed east as if it wanted no part of the aftermath.

Ned ejected his clip and slammed another in.

"Hold your fire!" I said getting up and we grouped.

Car lights and a couple of cop spotlights now beamed down on us and showed all the rubberneckers a right handsome display of smoking guns.

"Good luck surviving that one, kid!" Webb spit toward the prisoner.

Beans had a neck twice its size because his heart had climbed his esophagus. He looked at me and swallowed it back down. "Think of something, Lefty. Sell another sizzler to Deep Pockets!" he said. He spoke not in a yell or command, but rather a whisper, just loud enough for us to hear.

I looked around.

Rubberneckers and cops. Blue cop cars. White ones. Black and white cop cars too. It was like I was reading, Go Cop Go, to my great-grandkids. Cops were on the ground now, closing in, jumping car to car and then behind the corner of our V.F.W. They weren't stupid. They came in as the cover allowed, advancing slow, guns out for business.

Sirens grew and more cop spots cut the darkness, showing off our battle strewn property. Our WWII display was coming together.

The TV House didn't need to be spotlighted now. Beyond the rows of cops it was growing into a full blown fire.

Ned, Webb and Beans looked at me, stepping forward.

Spotlights lit us up like we were Nazi airplanes over London. They were yelling at us in a cop voices.

"Better keep our guns out," I said.

"You'll have to do better than that!" Ned said. I took a bullet or two." Blood dripped off the hand that held his gun. "Mines loaded, but I can't shoot."

"Can you dig the bullet out yourself?" I asked.

"I'll tell them it's a ricochet," Ned said

"They'll know it's from that popgun," Beans said. "We better blast our way out!"

"I can get the bullet," Ned said to prevent a shootout. "I can at least get one."

A cop voice now yelled with more tenacity for us to do something or another. It came from a megaphone.

"Think of something Lefty!" Beans said.

We were bunching together like turkeys on Thanksgiving as they surrounded us.

I looked at my buddies and felt an odd role, like I was now a designated liar. Nothing brilliant popped into my head. What could I say? 'They were dead when we got here?' That'd be a big fat help!

I dropped my .45 in the dirt. It was empty anyway and I pointed to the burning house, taking a step forward.

"Don't move soldier or we'll blow you to Christmas!" the megaphone barked at me. Great! We're going to get gunned down at our Post! Shot if we do, shot if we don't. We'll I suppose we deserved it for what we've done to those kids. Both now and then!

I looked at Beans.

He nodded. He believed in me.

That didn't help me. I knew the first one they'd shoot was the one who couldn't shoot back. At least that's what I always did back in the days of fires, bombs and explosions.

Ned motioned me to face the cops.

Christmas was looking better by the second. And more inevitable as they kept screaming. But I knew different. Christmas doesn't come to soldiers like us because God knows that good people don't win wars. Come to think of it, bad one's don't either!

I took a deep breath to stage some authority. "They went that way! Niptits!"

"Drop your weapons!" he yelled back.

"He's got a good point," Webb said, fingering his safety on, lowering his Thompson butt first and letting her go, barrel toward the danger.

Ned dropped his .45. Probably because it was too heavy to hold. The handle was red in blood. They should just make them that way. It's the color they always end up anyway.

I lifted my arm as if I could make them stop yelling. They were lathering themselves into a pretty good frenzy like those sharks in the China Sea when our Navy Men took their midnight dips.

I was glad Beans hadn't forfeited his weapon. With us pinned in the wide open and them behind their cars, I'd put my gold teeth on Beans gunhand any day. A part of me wanted to see how those kid cops could do with someone shooting back at them.

Webb eyed his Thompson.

I knew he'd drop to his belly and give it to them good. That drove me to either think of something or strip down for the bloodbath.

"Hey!" I yelled in my best victim voice. "Some kids stole one of our tanks!" I thumbed where it used to sit. "So we just got mad, and, shot the shit out this one!" I then pointed to the tank behind us, as I met their eyes. "What's the big deal?"

Beans nodded.

Webb too.

"Drop your pistol you little tin soldier!" the megaphone cop yelled.

I looked at Beans. That cop should not have said that. I bet he wasn't a trained negotiator.

Ned stepped away from Beans.

Webb did too, bumping into me and making me move back.

They started yelling at Beans full tilt.

"You first!" Beans held ground.

Good luck cops! I thought.

Shotguns racked shells from behind spotlights.

"You trying to scare me with a scattergun?" Beans yelled back. "I can fart those bullets away!"

Webb leaned over to me. "This outta be good."

I nodded.

They were far away. Behind cars doors and engine blocks as they yelled. That was pretty smart of them. They seemed to know what a .45 could do in sort range.

I turned looked at the tank, wondering if I could get behind it. I saw gray bullet scars across Webb's nice paint job. So much for our marksmanship.

"Look Webb," I nodded at the tank.

"What?"

"The slide is closed," I whispered.

Webb gawked. "Remind me never to play poker with that kid," he said. "He must be the slipperiest pussy in the cathouse."

25

The Battle Wanes

Me and Webb had a hard time turning our backs to Sherman County Prison. That Pal kid was still alive. Probably bleeding to death right now, but breathing nevertheless.

He was going to rat us out for killing his friend.

We turned back to the cops.

Beans dropped his .45 and they became the greater enemy.

Cops charged in and did their thing, backing us away from our Thunder Sticks, shoving us around then pushing us into the mud and then twisting us in knots.

Mud was mud. Pain was pain. I looked over at Beans who was closest.

He spit dirt out of his mouth. "Taste like chicken," he said to me, smiling.

Good ole Beans! You never really know where a man can find a smile!

When the thirty-odd cops finally found out they were bigger and stronger than us, they beamed their spotlights into the windows of our V.F.W. and took us inside where it was warmer.

We found ourselves in our chairs and the cards were on in the middle of the table called to us. But we stayed focus. Now was not a time for games. There was work to be done. Beans and Webb were still in handcuffs and I had to find a lie to save our lives.

Light from the road splashed against the far wall, keeping half our faces black in shadow.

I smiled at this two-faced look we all had, as I warmed up my forked tongue behind my teeth. I waited.

A Deputy slapped the back of my chair. "We don't buy it!"

"So, truth isn't for sale!" I said, sounding like every liar in the world.

"It don't figure," he leaned in like a tough cop from a 1955 movie.

"Hey! They stole our good tank, killing at least two people, and destroying who knows what. It's our fault! We should have never brought the tanks here for display."

"And you're big fence and high tech cameras and ground lighting? More's going on! And has been for quite a while!"

I looked at him.

He had a point there.

I put my hand on the table, then turned it palm up. "We thought they would detour people until we opened," I said. "We were wrong."

"So you get mad and shoot up the remaining tank?" another deputy said.

"Now you're putting the pieces together!" Beans said. "Atta boy!"

"Ouch," Ned said, looking hard at the EMS woman who had him seated, wrapping his shoulder.

"They're not at fault," Deep Pockets pointed to us, coming forward ahead of the sheriff boys. "Those punks are at fault!" he spoke into his shoulder mic, backing to the door.

"Now you're talking!" Beans said from behind a mask of mud. He must have sunk his face into it to get so much to stick. He jingled his cuffed wrist to the jailer.

"We've found the other tank!" Deep Pockets said and everyone looked at him as if he were the alpha hound in a fox hunt.

"Impressive," Webb said, holding out his wrist. "Shermans they do have a history of leaving a damage path."

"Not any more," Deep Pockets said.

"We shouldn't have gotten mad, but we didn't think anybody would steal a tank and go on a killing spree!" I said mainly for the benefit of keeping Beans and Webb from tangling up my lies.

All was quiet for a moment. Sheriff Deputies grouped in the hall. State Police lingered in the kitchen and Pockectville's Finest unlocked Beans and Webb.

Their town. Their mess. Their money.

Webb caught my eyes. "If the tank is down, it only means one thing."

The rest of looked at the cards.

I wanted to look out the window, but was nervous about having the light hit my whole face. Dumb cops or not, you don't mess around with light when you're a liar! I did catch a healthy orange glow from the TV house.

"It's on fire," Deep Pockets told me. He seemed to be curious too. "Fire trucks just got the water going. She'll be out soon."

Pal coughed as quietly as he could. On his back on the cool steel floor he felt beads of sweat grow on his forehead, roll down his temples and enter his hairline.

He was breathing better now, stacking breath upon breath. Something he didn't think was possible after his body got flat-bullet-upended and slammed into the tank walls as if a giant was shaking it. His body felt like a baseball knocked by a heavy hitter.

A part of him now wanted to yell out. To stand. To get rescued. To end it.

But the silent side of him won.

As he found his breath, he relaxed. Deft fingers now came up to his shoulder and felt how the bullet had opened it up. It hit him from the front, knocking him reeling. It seemed to come out the front too. He wondered how that could have happened.

His head must have hit a blunt wall when he was spun and his scalp was gashed. He now believed the blood he coughed out had come from his forehead and not up from his lungs, but he wasn't sure.

He didn't know how many bullets had come into the tank before he slammed the slide shut. It sounded like dozens.

He breathed, thankful that his lunges worked. Okay, he thought. I can do this. With a good chest I can survive this night. With his blood covered right hand, he made the sign of the cross just in case.

Knowing he couldn't stand helped him. His legs seemed very far away and he calmed himself and focused beyond all the tiresome screams and listened for the serious ones. He moved his toes. They worked. He bent both elbows. Even the one below his blasted shoulder worked. He bent up his left leg. It came up.

Pal smiled. The sound of lead, fragmenting and snarling about him was fading. It was a wicked, evil sound. The kind that would only satisfy a demon.

His working ear rang hard. The cool oil and sludge on the tank floor now felt like medicine on his age old burn wounds from the flare fire.

He went to bend his right knee and five, maybe six K-Bar knives seemed to stab and twist themselves under the kneecap. He tried to scream but there was no strength.

He saw color then. Bands purple and green came into the tank and he closed his eyes and fainted without even twitching. His clenched fists released their grip as he went out.

Gunfire woke Cell from the mud and smoke and he rolled, convulsing hard as his burned skin fused with super-heated Kevlar. He sat to escape heat. His hand went to his head and tried to shoo away Tonto, who was slicing away at the scalp with a tomahawk. There seemed to be a volleyball lodged between his skin and skull.

Fire grew to flame and Cell stood. All was dark around him, but light seemed to be shooting overhead. A thick light. One that seemed tangible.

The roll the thunder gunfire had ceased. Echoing rumbles ran away into the night. He turned in a small circle like a mouse in a radiation experiment.

The tank came back to him. He saw it fall into his house.

His mother.

He turned.

Seeing her about him sent a poison into his guts and he vomited as if to save his life. He tried to turn away, but some sprayed on her nevertheless. Some sizzled on hot embers.

On hands and knees, he crawled away from the advancing fire, following the contours of darkness, along the shadows of debris until he made it up a wall. Seeing a forest ahead of him, he wormed for it as lights cut the night until spotlights focused on the VFW across the way.

He remembered the men who had stood before him. He saw himself enraged and charging.

They're still over there! This powered him to crawl hard and low for the darkness. Survival depended on it.

Safe behind trees, he fought the urge to run. He stood and looked around.

Cops had the soldiers.

A small, subtle smile came to Cell's grime and blood-covered face. The smile soon left as he wiped it to a scowl with the back of his wrist.

He watched the cops charge and knock the VFW geezers into the mud.

Cell nodded. "Reep it!" he smiled, then turned and walked north. Away from the scene and into the thick of the lowland swamps he went.

It was cold. He was soaked and burned nearly to the bone, but he felt nothing as he walked except his own blood, pumping hard through his body. He walked north, because for the first time in his life, he knew where he was going.

26

FLOOD OF DEATH

Splinter dove through the debris hole first and he drowned in a convulsing, tangled mesh like spinning, gagging crocodile.

This saved Red's life, who took a few moments to gather his thoughts. As he drifted towards the big warm place, he seemed at peace as he shuddered away pieces of red ice from his body, sending continuous tiny red waves across the water. His head and torso found their way onto the numbing steel slab, inches out of the water and he found rest. His body temperature started to drop a degree or so every few minutes. Soon his shivering stopped trying to wake up his externals as the blood focused on the major organs.

He then stopped breathing altogether in the cold, red world of ice and water at the bottom of McLarry's pond.

Red never heard the bubbles or the metal grating sound or saw a faint yellow glow when Pocketville's one diver, shivering inside his drysuit, hooked cables to the tank.

Weight and mass, diluted by the pressure of water, allowed the the tow trucks to winch the tank through bottom muck after they had strapped themselves to large trees to help hold their ground.

Steal groaned and men stepped away. Lights on generators beamed across McLarry's pond. Cable cut through the ice, breaking it to burgs. The barrel of the Sherman came topside first, then the right side of the machine.

"Stop! Halt!" men yelled. Winching came to a sudden jolt and squeal of stretched metal relaxed.

I looked at Webb.

Webb had insisted he come since it was his property that had been stolen. He looked back at me.

We both saw the boy stuck in the debris net of wire, fence, wood and branches. His carcass was white in the muddy waters and fire rescue dove into the pond.

"Too little too late," I said to Webb. We were alone now. Except for death. Us and death were again in a dance.

"Good luck helping that one," Webb said. "Unless they can walk of water. And ice doesn't count," he added in case I was in the mood to challenge his theology.

Like I had time for that.

We stayed still. We knew what death looked like already. Better let others get a feel for it. We had been tooting ours around for too long.

They took away the dead kid in a bag.

We heard it get zipped shut. Unique sound.

Duel winches started working above us again and we walked away, putting distance between us and the straining cables. One doesn't just haul a tipped over tank ashore with the flip of a switch.

Half the tank made it up the bank before the power failed on the tow trucks. Water poured out and a man beamed a flashlight inside after others had pulled aside wreckage.

"We got another!" the rescuer yelled.

I looked at Webb. A twofer.

His eyes stayed on his tank.

The body we knew as Red came out.

Webb grunted and looked at me. "Beans should have come. He would have liked this!"

"Nice of him to stay with Ned," Webb said. "And they need to get that bullet out."

I looked at my watch and stomped my feet in the snow to move blood. "They're playing by now."

Red went to a stretcher and someone started hitting his chest and giving him CPR.

"A lot of good that will do," I said. "Do they know something we don't?" I recalled the chances I had to save men. Felt their heated blood on my arms. Winced as their scared fingers dug into my flesh. Went sad as I remembered lying to them, saying they would be okay, that sawbones was coming to patch them back together.

I knew I had my chances to save men so I just watched other take theirs.

I shook my head. One gets a lot of those kind of chances when war rears its head from the mud and decides to slither on the topside turf. After all, war lives in the place where we all have come from. It lives in the dirt, far from the breath of God. It thrives in the darkness of the forsaken human heart.

Meal Tab stepped back from the ice, cinched up his pants and pointed up the hill to us. Then he waved us down.

We stayed still. It was dark after all.

Then he sent Deep Pockets of fetch us so we came.

"Recognize them?" Meal Tab asked, nodding toward the bag near the boy getting CPR.

"We've seen those bags before. Seen more than the factory fows who make them in the first place."

"I'm talking about the boys," Meal Tab said.

"Unzip it," Webb said.

Deep Pockets did and a white, frosty face appeared.

We shook our heads. "They from around here?"

"Ya."

"Sure?" I asked.

Meal Tab looked at Deep Pockets and nodded.

Deep Pockets let go of the zipper and stood. "Take another look," he said.

We did, then looked back at him.

"We questioned these two about their missing buddy a couple of weeks ago. They said he took off out west," Pay Tabb said.

Me and Webb looked at each other then back at them. That was news to us. We didn't know anything about Pal saying he was going west. The last we knew of Pal is that we shot him dead inside the other tank.

"Take another look," Deep Pockets said with some toughness.

We did. We looked good and long as the shaggy blond corpse. Good thing too. Looking at the ground is good. It hides one's guilt until he can get his wits about him.

I looked up at Meal Tab.

"What are you saying, Meal Tab?" I asked.

"I'm saying there's a lot of death going on around your VFW!"

I looked over at Webb, then back at the chief and shrugged my shoulders. He had a good point there.

27

CELL'S ESCAPE

Cell kept tripping across the dark forest floor until he found a stick. It was a small tree rather, so he swung it against a trunk a few time until it broke in half. Then using the club end of the rod, he managed cross the wood to the converted bike path.

Twenty minutes later, he stood alone in the middle of the dark road in front of the house of Old Man Jones. Clothes burnt black, hair singed down to his scalp and blood oozing and drying across half of his face, he stared at the house. With his pause, came screams of pain and stiffness. His bone burnt right arm seemed to be missing its meat.

A frigid March chill tried to cool him, but Cell now had inner fire and this drove him to his duty.

Something rotten stung at his nose and irritated him. It re-routed his fragile bloodflow, and upset his balance. It diverted him to look down at his feet and he saw a cat, half decomposed into the asphalt.

Big Berta was right.

Jones was a cat killer.

Cell looked up and down the road. And was still. He looked south where Deep Pocket & Company were circling multiple crime scenes, tooting their sirens and running red and blue lights. He wondered if they had found his mother. Turning, he gripped his stick and scraped up cold roadkill of rawhide and fur. Stiff from winter, meat and innards were still intact.

Holding the critter by its hind legs, he walked toward the Jones door and eyed the cat traps on the porch.

On Jones window ledge sat a half role of gray tape and Cell matched it to the weather-beaten repairs to the cat traps.

Cell stepped onto the porch and it creaked. I light came on in the living room. It was a lamp and chair level and Pal heard footsteps coming.

Stomping twice on the steps, he shrieked out his best tortured meow.

The door opened and old man Jones eyes were bright as he looked to his traps.

Cell brought the club down on the man's head, knocking him to the wooden planking of the porch.

The man moaned and Cell kicked him in the stomach and heard frail ribs cave in. The boy leaned down and glared at the old man by his feet.

The man's eyes were wide and dancing in horror.

"Fear this!" Cell took his stick and put it to the man's neck and applied pressure, forcing the man's tongue to leave its mouth.

"You a tough killer, huh?" Cell asked and readied himself to raise the club and finish it. Then he eyed the traps. Stepping hard on the man's arm, he bent and pulled up a box trap with his club. He then put a knee in the old man's chest and bent up the fragile elbow.

Old man Jones was weak and dazed. Pain of ribs stabbing his heart and lungs made his eyes sweat. He saw the traps coming to him and flexed muscle to fight it off, but those days had gone. He saw the trap come up and clenched his fist as the box went over his hand.

Steel tripped and the trap sprung, snapping itself from Cell's grip as it bit down.

With the stick off his neck, Jones could scream if he could only breath. He inhaled.

Branches across the road seemed to sway as Jones haunting, eerie moan sang out its sad song of hand torture, chest trauma and a splitting skull ache.

"Welcome to a night of sin," Cell said and took the other trap and forced the man's other arm into it.

Bent steel snapped and he distinctly heard bones crack as the man eicked out another wailer. Then the tired lungs gave way to a withering agony.

Cell stepped off the man and raised his club, pausing until the old man's eyes could open.

Jones saw him and brought up both box hands to ward the blow.

He picked up the decayed cat and dropped it on Jones face and took up the gray tape. He gauged his energy against the distance to Berta's animal clinic and the house just beyond where she lived.

Then he finished the job and walked away in the direction of proper medical care. Behind him on the porch was a bench held by chains from the ceiling. On it swung a seated man that could scare more than a crow. It had boxes for hands and a dead cat for a face.

Beans and Ned looked at the small caliber, blood painted bullet on the table. It glowed red because bright, generator powered lights of Pocketville Fire Department had the VFW interior illuminated.

The two men were alone. Holding down the fort one might say.

Wendell and Lefty were on recon, gathering enemy information once again.

Beans looked at the monitors out of habit but they were still dark, juiceless. On his lap was his other .45, the first being impounded by Deep Pockets. But the safety was on and nothing was racked.

Things appeared to be dying down.

Beans wasn't fooled by the stillness. He hadn't ever been fooled in the company of the dead. He had always killed the dead. That's why he was still alive. Now Beans closed his eyes and saw water exploding from chest of Jap Nappers. The only ones he didn't shoot at were the ones who had no chest to begin with. Ammunition well spent was his model. It was the one thing they had plenty of.

A blood-tipped Leatherman utility tool was in front of Ned. It held back a small hill of gold teeth like a steel dam.

Beans held three cards and pulled in two more. He dropped a gold tooth next to the bullet.

"It's mine. Mere cards can't stop that," Ned said.

"I pulled it out," Beans laid down a pair of eights. King high.

Ned dropped two aces and took up his bullet and another gold tooth and dropped them to rest in a larger grouping next to his tool. Popping the top off an aspirin bottle, he dry-crunched and swallowed a few more pills, lips wincing.

"Aces and eights," Beans smiled, showing white lines in the mud cracks on his face. "It's about time."

Along the north property line of the animal clinic, sat a sleepy, walkout ranch style house like a church parsonage. Once inside, Big Berta's enjoyed quiet evenings, only bothered once, maybe twice a week by calls of protective pet owners and, of course, a monthly drama usually caused by a hair ball.

So when Big Berta got rousted up by an insensate doorbell ringing, she hit the front lights. For some reason her skin seemed to rise on her back, so she took up her greased polished cast iron frying pan as she passed through her kitchen.

Her clients used phones.

She opened the door with a push, looked beyond the Beirut Bombed Boy, then stepped back and waved him in. She remembered him not so much as Red's friend, but as the one who said he'd take care of Old Man Jones and his cat traps. She gauged his trauma with a off-centered stare and turned him to the kitchen. Then she looked across her property, closed her door and flipped off her front lights.

Berta sat her weapon back on the stove and spun a faucet. Steam rose from the sink.

"Old Man Jones do this to you?"

Cell scoffed, remembering how the weak chest caved in. Maybe I kicked him too hard. Maybe I should have hit army vets harder. Duh, he thought. "No," he said.

"So you took care of the traps?" she asked, gauging the boy's lacerations in a long, absorbing scan.

"Jones too!" Cell winced as she opened his vest, separating it from burned muscle. He smelled burnt flesh. It stung his nose like the meals his mom burnt during commercials. "He irritated me."

"What happened?"

"He was in his house and..."

"Not to him! You think I care about a cat killer?"

"To me?"

She nodded.

He nodded back. That was nice. Not many people had asked him about himself. "Well, about an hour ago, me and my friends were..."

"Start from the beginning," she said. "Untangling this will take more than one story."

She opened the back door and they walked out into the night. A cool wind stirred the leaves by their feet as they tread a well worn path that connected her home to her business. It was still dark when they went inside the side door and he followed her through some dark rooms until they came to small operating room.

Cell cleared his throat and watched a needle poke through a white spot on his arm, cleaned by alcohol swabs. Minutes later his words and stories rolled from his tongue and all was well.

After burn cream layered the side of his body he was still mumbling.

She knew his arm should receive a skin graph, but the procedure would leave a mark. Up to now she had done what a brainless pharmacist at Pocketville DrugMart could do.

Cell had quieted after a dozen rolls of white gauze wrapped his torso, leg and arm.

She shot X-Rays of his chest and knew his cracked rib must have caused some howling.

He now looked around and realized that he had been moved into a surgical room at the clinic. She had a cool cloth on his head.

"How'd I get here?"

"I carried you," she lied. She knew he wouldn't remember anything anyway.

"Pal got us to take the tank. Only not me," Cell said.

"Pal's the prisoner in the other tank, right?" she asked.

He nodded.

"And he's good with me helping you?"

"Oh ya! He pushed Red to take Splinter here for his finger."

"That's right," she said, opening another sterile pad.

"We were going to crush the VFW and get 'em good!" his eyes faded off. "But all we got was my mom!"

All went quiet and his eyes started needling something fierce. Next he found himself weeping against her. He felt her arms around him and the softness of her chest, sappy with his tears.

He sat upright and grunted away from her, groaning as he made himself lay back down on the metal surgical table. Once there, he fainted again with the image of them holding each other as his mind worked to swirl it away like the dust and exhaust stirred up by the tank in his basement.

Berta didn't have much experience with extreme electrical burns and, to her embarrassment, found herself reading up on burns at WebMD. She worried about the boy's arm and chest, fearing infection. She told him how she had cared for the wounds, but she didn't think he was the type who could sell the story that he patched himself up to Deep Pockets.

After he passed out the second time, she took up her remote and clicked the TV on. She preferred animals to liars.

Critters don't barf up tall tree tales to scam a veterinarian to get illegal medical attention.

Berta knew boy's like Cell lived in a foam rubber world. She remembered high school with a frown. Boy's like Cell were the ones who passed out puking at the party porcelain and got their faces kicked in by every person who had to take a piss.

She looked over at the Cell and shook her head and smiled. If she had a nickel for every client's guilty story she'd would now be prying war nickels away from coin collectors.

Her TV came on and all three Grand Rapids News stations were covering Cell's story. Her head turned left and saw her Veterinary Medical Degree. Next to it was framed her practicing license. Her head tilted and she looked at Cell. Her hand shook as it pressed the volume on the remote. Since when to TV and reality co-exist?

Berta left Cell on the table with no railings and walked to her front door and looked south. Beyond the tree line, maybe two miles away, she could hear the helicopters running live feed to the news crews at McLarry's Pond. She looked back at her TV and confirmed this.

She glanced north and south and closed the door and doused the clinic lights.

In the blue glow of her TV, she surfed up to CNN. They were covering a suicide in Hollywood. Turning to FOX News, she frowned.

FOX News ran and re-ran the image of a WWII Sherman Tank being winched from McLarry's Pond.

Pocketville had gone primetime!

Bimbo Blondie of Grand Rapids was getting her moment in mayhem as she fed the big boy live. Finger in her ear, she answered questions on the tank drivers. One dead in a body bag. EMS team striving to save the other.

While she talked, FOX ran damage path footage.

Hopefully Red's in the bag, Berta thought. She went to her clinic windows and looked outside once again. Satisfied on the stillness, she retreated to the TV.

The camera panned along the damage path and now settled on a crater.

"So that's your house!" she said to her unconscious patient. She saw the other Sherman tank in the parking lot at the VFW.

And there's the prisoner tank! She thought

Berta looked back at Cell. Then looked around her clinic.

If those tales are true, then Old Man's Jones got himself beaten and trap-snapped to death. Cat wretch is taped to his face!

I'm an accomplice to Murder One, Aiding and Abetting, Practicing Medicine without a license, harboring a fugitive. Oh Pumkin Patch these kids! Deep Pockets will make get sixty charges on me!

Berta looked at Cell, TV light turning his white gauze blue. That poor child.

Cell moaned in pain and Berta dipped a needle into another bottle. One more injection was needed to calm him. He was a good kid. He deserved to be calmed.

She left the sleeping boy and returned with a stainless table on wheels she used for moving the Nelson's Newfoundlands after they got spayed.

Rolling Cells body from the table to the cart, she rolled the boy down the dark hallway to her crematorium.

"He'll fit," she said over the sound of a wobbling left back wheel. "He'll fit just fine."

28

SCHEMING & HEALING

Dungy was happier than jack rabbit at a Cialis Convention. He pushed up his glasses on his forehead and looked at his computer screen. It was after midnight, two days after carnage. He wasn't tired. He was breaking great stories, making the world go around, and getting paid for it!

The Pocketville Triangle had sold copy to the Associated Press! And now AP wanted more.

Knowing he helped stage the struggle by giving front page turf to the flagpole saboteurs, gave him a sense of status. And he took his responsibility serious.

Brance at Pocketville Hardware was his secret informant, not because of credibility, but because of sell-ability. Brance was farthest to the right on a paranoia theory. It might be too fetchy for Hollywood but not the syndicated press.

The Deep Pocket Pals weren't commenting, citing ongoing investigation, but they nodded in agreement to a few of Dungy's insight, giving verification without revealing proof.

And sensational it was!

The punk-muckers Splinter, Cell, Pal and Red had matured their purpose and had set out to combine gang activity and terrorism.

Gang activity always yielded a higher exchange rate than terrorism locally.

Brance showed Dungy surveillance tapes of all four teenagers buying potato guns the day before Wendell had supposable fallen on the VFW steps. "The VFW has a ramp," Brance had said.

But Duke Dungy needed more. His subscribers deserved it. He dug deep into overtime, not interested in connecting a string of cute dots like lights on a Christmas tree. He wanted to focus all the hype and build a beam of light like a lazer.

But thus far the magical connection was still hidden from him. Maybe there wasn't one. Maybe it was Redneck who just started there sentences with, 'Hey, watch this!"

Duke doubted this.

His copy of the Missing Child Report was left of center on his desk. It was for a 17 year old boy, filed by two frantic parents who had convinced him that their kid wasn't the cross-country hitchhiker like his letter had said.

"He left his wallet," his father had said.

"Any money in it?" Dungy had asked.

"Eighty bucks."

Dungy believed them and they started crying.

Pal didn't run away.

Dungy tapped the report. He believed Pal was dead. Hopefully murdered. He wanted a mug shot of a kid killer from the cops. Any crime photo would be nice. And another dead body would solidify a three thousand readership mark two weeks in a row.

The Death Report next to Pal's MIA was of the wailing kid at the coffin. DOA in the capsized tank. Choked on wire. Duke liked the coroner's report. Nothing fancy except a missing finger injury that wasn't recorded by Pocketville's six doctors or the ER's in downtown or Five County Hospital. And a side note reported a finger infection on his opposite hand. Same finger as the missing one. Splinter had pinky problems. The examiner speculated self-mutilation.

Dungy doubted that. The dead boy's mother had breakfast with Duke in a private room at Slender's Bar and Grill where she was a cocktail waitress. "It's his only passion," she said. "He ain't going to mess with his fingers because that all that connects him to his reality."

"What reality?" he asked.

"Video Game Wars," she said. "And of course, stupid me! I kicked them out of my house or none of this would have happened."

"Why?"

"Lost my temper."

"What made you do that?"

She looked around.

Duke bit his lip, holding back assumptions and hoping for the missing piece.

"They shot up my dog with paintballs," she said.

Duke hid his disappointment.

"Listen to me! Those boys met someone in battle out their in The Web and he's come to Pocketville. He's killing all of them!"

Dungy reported this to the Sheriff. They had the resources to research this. It seemed viable, but Dungy hoped it wasn't. What he needed was a homegrown serial killer. A real monster. Imported ones were a dime down the paper shredder. A True Blue Michigan Maniac is what the Triangle needed. The Associated Press needed it too. They requested it specifically. He felt the pressure.

Pocketville Police didn't buy the Internet Killer Theory. It cost too much. They were too busy filing charges against Red, the boy rotting in a coma over at County Five Hospital. A Deep Pocket was outside his door twenty-four seven. Pocketville's finest needed Red alive to collect charges and damage fees. Currently they had seventeen, but word was out that more were in the mixer.

That sounded high to Dungy. Even for Deep-Pocketville that seemed high. He planned to publish the list if the kid woke up. That might be enough to send him back to bed.

Duke stood next to his journalism desk, paced and shook his head. Something was needed if the four-thousand mark was going to happen. He looked at the dead kid again. Then he dug through his computer and pulled up digitals pics of the funeral. He had learned from the Bill and Monica Lewinsky White House Washers that a photo journalist should never erase pics. He had hard drives full of them. Dated chronologically so they would always be somewhere.

He found the one he wanted. Enlarged it and printed it off. A one-handed veteran as old as time was shaking the hand of Splinter. That boy wasn't crying from heartache! Splinter was juicing it up because his fingerless hand was being crunched in a handshake!

With the hand inside a coat, how did the veteran know it was fingerless? How did he know where to grab?

Duke looked at the phone and wanted to call someone. But he turned to the shredder instead and sent the photo into a better place, obeying the first law of journalism. Don't let anyone else get the money, honey.

He turned to the Emergency Room notes from Wendell and then at the calendar. They just looked wrong to him. Too clean. Too perfect. He checked a number of his ambulance chaser and left him a vague message with just enough sauce to get a call back. If something was wrong on the hospital report, the chaser would find it.

Now Dungy picked up the other Missing Person Report. It was of Cell. Not filled by his mother since she had been pancaked beyond public policy by a Sherman Tank. Dungy frowned. Too bad. He was still missing the perfect picture. He was thinking about her high school photo being run underneath a Sherman Tank photo, but had not yet become a believer. Plus she was a Trailer Trash Can Ma'am. She couldn't get a reader to lick a finger.

Pocketville Police had ordered the autopsy on Cell's Mom and it was seventy-nine pages long.

Dungy hoped her kid would never get a chance to read it. It made Dungy sick. Despite feeling that Deep Pockets gouged the system with a twenty-six hour autopsy bill, he liked the indisputable evidence that a person had actually gotten ran over by a WWII tank in his journalism beat. Without her corpse, AP wouldn't have picked up the story.

TV helicopter cameras captured the footage before cops got blankets over her. FOX was still debating running it after 9 p.m. with a viewer discretion. They bought the exclusive rights for the footage for an undisclosed amount.

Dungy sat back down. Two missing person's reports, for two kids in a group of four. A death certificate for the third and the forth in a comma.

Brance's theory of old timers in a private war at the VFW was getting stronger.

But he had met with the old timers yesterday. That was twice in as many weeks. He didn't feel it. He felt they were irritated because they couldn't play poker in peace. He looked for chips but couldn't find any. He sensed they had the patience of Job.

Dungy rubbed fingers in his temples and looked at the Police Report for Sigmund Jones on the north side.

On any other day, such a hate crime would have been front and center with the cat traps and duct tape carcass mashed into a face. Duke could have milked it for month.

A bad way to go. Duke thought. A lot of ugly out there. Lot of ugly. Too bad ugly doesn't sell papers.

Dungy needed evil. He needed to find the source powering up the violent, inhuman, sociopathic and a loose reckless hate that would make a reader buy more paper.

Too bad Jones didn't have a computer or a history of internet stalking. But either way he was too old and soft for the violence. So were the veterans for that matter.

And the way Jones was murdered didn't fit with the dipsy dotsy rhythm of the Teen Ring. Not that Dungy was looking a gift horse in the mouth. Any murder meant a one thousand boost in papers sold.

But what Dungy needed was the intolerance beneath the hate. Dungy needed the source of evil so it could inspire Pocketvillians to seek knowledge with a passion. To buy papers by the dozen. If he could find that, he could have the Associated Press eating from his hand.

Dungy pushed the Jones Hate Crime Report to the right. He needed these crimes to be more spread out so he could pull in longterm readership from other towns. With everything happening all at once it just looked like Drano was in the dipsticks. Despite his efforts, he couldn't yet see how Pocktetville was different than any other town.

Not yet.

But he felt it was there. It had to be. The pot of Associated Press Gold always spilled on towns that produced crimes that have never happened before in the history of America.

He poured himself another cup of coffee and reviewed his stacks.

A two week old, Missing Persons Report on a kid called, Pal.

An All Points Bulletin on a Missing Person called, Cell.

Two week old, Death Certificate on WWII Veteran, Wendell.

Death Certificate on Cell's fat mom.

Death Certificate on Cell's friend, Splinter.

Death Certificate on an old man called, Jones.

Dungy looked at the TOD's. Time of Deaths. All with minutes of each other but for Wendell. Unrelated my beat!

He looked at his cup of coffee, half filled with cream and sugar and shook his head. It was a sorry day for Pocketville Triangle when Duke Dungy couldn't stay ahead of the Deep Pocket Patrollers.

Wait. Wasn't their four boys in the gang? He looked at his stack. Oops. Forgot the one at County Five Hospital. Dungy looked at the clock. Sleep would be good. Real good.

He sat. He would just do a little digging. Splinter's that break dams always got churned up by the beaver with the smallest teeth. Get it? Splinter? He looked at his clock. It was going to be a long night if his inner voice got talking.

Pal awoke and the tank was lit by one of four flashlights that had been tapped together and dropped inside. He took hold of it and his hand shook hard, dancing the light into a sack of medicine and food. Sitting upright, he snapped open the Stiletto™ from the bag and opened the gauze as the razor slipped between his padding and skin.

Dried, green and yellow puss had caked the wrapping and the bandages held the mass until it was released. It fell in a near splat onto the rag pile on the tank floor.

Breaking the seal on another small bottle of peroxide, he poured it onto his knee, gripping the hand hold on the wall before doing so. Colors of green and pink came before his eyes, surfing the pain, but he stayed upright.

That was a first. He had passed out in pain during his other two clean-ups. He took up the third of a dozen tubes of Neosporin from the sack and emptied it on the opening below the kneecap.

He saw how his white ligament, as wide as his tongue, had been severed, cut in half like a hallway carpet. As told by the instruction in the paper sack, he bit down on jerky as he did the cleaning procedures.

Inside his knee somewhere was a .45 slug, described by the medical notes to be as flat as a silver dollar. His medical kit had come the night of his shootout.

His buddies had survived the tank and were still free! He admired how they infiltrated the compound to save his life.

Details inside that med kit told him how to cheat death. The basics on bullet removal and survival. A jug of green tea had come with it. It tasted like piss. And some crushed herbs were to be sprinkled on his wounds. He didn't know how Red knew this, but Red was resourceful. Splinter too.

Infection in his knee started pouring out after his first cleansing.

Blood on the open shoulder wound now seemed to be dried and hard. He stopped touching it because it was healing, just like he was told.

Pal figured the pack had come from Berta. At this he smiled, recalling how Splinter had tried to be brave in front of her as Red stitched up the finger nub.

He hadn't heard from any of them since they drove off in the tank. Not hearing from Cell was a gimme.

Pal shuddered, remembering the streetlights flickering in power drain. He shuddered in his delirium. To his knowledge, he didn't remember Cell killing a veteran with a potato gun and shooting them up with a six gun.

No, he thought. I attacked them. And they're going to kill me!

Now Pal sat and took a few bits of food. Jerky and dried fruit that had been dumped into his hatch. Somehow he thought Berta was more of fresh vegetable person, being a woman and all. Not that he was complaining. He enjoyed how his lungs could inhale and exhale.

Pal looked around. He had to take a crap. He nodded. Taking a crap was a good sign. It was his first one after getting shot two days ago.

29

NED LEAVES

Meal Tab looked across six coffee pots and four brunchers from two competing bakeries and a deli. Beyond the beverages sat his team minus one, because they patrolled the comatose redneck at County Five Intensive Care.

Red's father had just left. A sad, tired old man who seemed to have blown up every relationship in his life, except between him and his father, who he had to get back home and watch over.

The father was old school. Guilty as a Detroit rat and taking it to the grave with him. "The truck burned up out at the VFW belonged to my boy!" he said, making one newsworthy point. It went against five outstanding service men who said it was abandoned, but it was recorded nevertheless.

Off to the left sat the Sheriff Scat. They didn't seem to care which way the mess went because they weren't in it for the money.

Pocketville was. Damage fees were mounting and he needed a piece of the pie if he was going to pay for the inline cameras across his town.

In front of Meal tab sat the folders. State Farm wanted Victim Compenstaion on the dead woman's house. Her insurance company had ordered a copy of the autopsy, citing suspicion. Owners of the three poles barns mucked up by tank had all filed insurance and restitution claims. One had housed a classic car and it only had Parade insurance on them. The Electric Company had lost entire electric grid, two transformers and a mile of string. Gas Company and the Cable Company were violated. Department of Transportation was still assessing some road damage, tentative figures could hit one million because the tank cracked a bridge on it's way to the McLarry bog. Pocketville Towing and Hauling, Fire Department, Pocketville Ambulance had sent all three units and well as two First Responders Teams, Emergency Management Specialist, State Police, Sheriff's Department, Department of Natural Resources, Grand Rapids Special Weapons and Tactics team and the Bomb Squad also had claims coming.

Departement of Alcohol, Tobacco and Firearms had gotten wind of the turmoil and their West Michigan man in charge put the Michigan National Guard on alert status, launching three A-10 Tank Killers from up in Graying.

Chief scratched his scalp. That included over fifty men in one lousy call.

Federal Bureau of Investigatin now had a man in the room because Missing Children was punishable beyond the State of Michigan. Amber Alerts had been active on Cell for two days.

Meal Tab shoulders slumped and he took in more coffee. The paper work was going to be astronomical and the idea of hiring an independent clerk service from the Feds looked more appealing by the moment. He knew he wouldn't get as big as slice if he outsourced the problem and was currently mulling over the idea of keeping it internal to control the profits.

Something like this only happened once in a career. He could do it. He had some good people around him.

Ned didn't look good. And it wasn't because he lost his red bullet to Webb, who also cleaned him out of eight gold teeth. He was pale, running a fever and his silver dollar had come out and was walking across his knuckles.

"I am on antibiotics, you fools!" he yelled, slamming his hand down. "You don't think I can't write my own way?"

I knew he couldn't. And I didn't blame him for being angry. I'd go eight teeth on full house. None of us had been dealt a flush since the War Monger years.

Ned pulled the glass thermometer out from under his tongue and held it to the light. He swore.

"What?" we asked, well beyond fine print.

"I'm losing the last of my brain cells."

"What's that mean?"

"It's septicemia men," Ned said.

"English Cap'n," Webb said.

Beans looked at me and shook his head. He seemed to know.

"Blood poisoning," Ned said

"Take something else," Webb said. "A doctors got to get in on this."

`"I'm a doctor," Ned said.

"It's not what I mean," Webb said. "We need to get you in."

"Look at this," Ned held up his thumb.

We all leaned in.

"Nicked my thumb nail yesterday. No biggie," he touched his thumbnail and took it clean off like the Asians did to all their fresh prisoners. He dropped it on the table and we watch some gloop come out from the raw area on his thumb. We didn't need glasses for that.

"That's not worth betting on," Beans said. "You're just a sore loser."

"It's blood poisoning," Ned said. "My blood is infected with bacteria, collecting at every knick and nack."

"What's it mean?" I asked.

"A day. Maybe two," Ned said.

We looked around. That didn't sound good.

"They'll cut me open and find the bullet in my guts," Ned said. "The other .22."

"Well that's nice of you to tell us now," I said. "Beans, I assume you knew of this!"

"So," Beans said. "Ned's law. Not mine. When you go out you can make your own laws. Me too. It's the only thing we can do anymore with dignity. Declare how we die and be damned."

"Watch your language on damnation, Beans." Webb said. "It's a wise choice to respect God during these days."

Ned looked around the table at us. Then he eyed our Nazi teeth.

I had twenty.

Beans thirty-six.

Webb had over fifty. He was killing us.

Before Ned was an empty table. "I'm dying with a dollar to my name," he said, letting the silver clink on the table. "Feds aren't going to get rich off me."

I took up the cards and shuffled one-handed in a way that would cause envy in a Vegas dealer. Then I dealt. "Well, you're not dead yet. What are you thinking of doing."

"Dunno. It ain't sitting well what I did. Rolling fatso and cooking him on the wires."

"You mean not killing him?" Beans asked.

"You tell me? How come he's not dead?" Ned shook his head. "I can't even kill anymore. Do you know how emasculating it is, knowing you can't even kill?"

"He's dead somewhere," Webb said. "He hobbled off into the woods and Deep Pockets was too busy counting coins or they would have called in their K-9's."

"We killed that Jones fellar, then, didn't we?" Ned said. "We know fatso did it. He could make it that far, that little Crème-Filled, Krispy Critter.

"So Jones is dead because all of us," Webb said. "Get over it!" he held up two fingers and I slide him the cards. "If we think only soldiers die in a war, we're more senile than we look."

"You know the man?" Ned asked.

We shook our heads.

Beans took only one card. "Play out the game, Ned. Wendell's dead. Their skinny is dead. Blacky's dying in prison. Fatso's missing. And the Redneck is rotting in the hospital. We're still sleeping at night. We're still winning the war."

I looked at Webb and Ned. None of us were sleeping that good.

After the game we walked out into the night. The lights were out and we stood in moonlight. The fence mesh pile was behind us, our flagpole in the mud before us. One tank was a prison, the other reeked of dead fish and pond bottom mud.

Webb had locked the hatch shut to get Deep Pockets off the grounds.

Ned stood next to his truck because we held him up. His hair was matted like South Pacific sweat. He grunted as we lifted him into his truck.

Beans gave him a canteen and Ned nodded hard to him. "I've always liked you Beans. You shared your salt with me and kept me alive after my Mrs. died. I want you to know that."

Beans nodded.

"Where you going?" Webb asked.

I looked hard at Webb. Let him go in peace! I thought. I looked at Ned. It would be nice to know.

"And don't think that I could respect another person more than you, Beans," Ned said. "You know this, but I'm saying it anyways. How you handled Bataan was a miracle. You're beyond what science can do, Beans. And if a drop of your blood was in me now, I'd be back playing cards."

"You can have some if you think it'll help," Beans said. He didn't like saying good bye. Not to a life long friend.

None of us did, but we did it anyway.

Ned looked at Webb. "The blood of God's son wouldn't help me now. Not after the things we've done."

"Now you're telling me to give up my hope?" Webb asked. "You need to go. Don't mess with a man's hope."

Ned turned his key to let his diesel glow plug warm. "I'm not messing with your hope, Webb. And you got enough to go around if I did."

I took a step forward.

He started the truck and looked at me.

"I'm going to my cabin, Lefty. I always liked it up there," he said.

"Good choice," I said. "When it warms we'll take care of you."

"I'll be in the cabin, waiting," Ned said.

"Take care," Beans said.

"Appreciate it," Ned said. "Letting me do this, I mean. You're soldiers. Then and now."

Ned drove off into the night.

It wasn't necessary for him to tell the three of us that. We have always done what dying men have asked.

We went back inside and sat at the card table.

Webb collected the cards.

We looked at Ned's thumbnail.

"I say that's worth about five gold teeth," Beans said.

We nodded. Five sounded about right.

30

PRISONER RELEASE

Duke Dungy visited Berta at her animal clinic. He took in a puppy called, Flipsy; his neighbors Shiatsu-Poodle.

"They want me to adopt it," he said to Berta when they met. "You know me, if things are too good to be true, well, you know. I think it has worms."

"Duke Dungy, huh. Sounds familiar."

"I'm with the Pocketville Triangle. Do you subscribe?" he asked and smiled, sensing that he was being out-sniffed. Why is she sniffing my butt? Duke looked at the mutt and shut up. He kept twirling his finger in the canine's neck scuff. He knew she was staring at him. Well, let her stare. I can be an animal lover for a few moments. He kept his eyes down. If she found he was here because Red's mom was her business partner, he'd get sent out the door like a puppy that piddled on her carpet.

"Do you have worm, Flipsy?" Duke asked the dog. Duke had a great job because he was always looking for answers from people who didn't want to give them.

"Shoddles are a good mix so you'll do well by it. And worms are a dog's best friend."

Duke looked up as she spoke.

"None shedding drives their price up. She's like a Daisy and can fetch five hundred to a thousand from a picky buyer. Yuppies. Clean freaks. Parents with asthma kids. But they don't call them Shiatsus for nothing. Hard to potty train. They seem to enjoy watching humans wipe up their little crappers." Berta pulled back the gums and looked at the dog's teeth.

The puppy screeched.

"Oh, quite your whining!" Berta said.

"So you think it's a good dog?"

"Dog? That's a good one! If you believe evolution is a mutation that results in a weaker species, you got yourself all the proof you'll ever need."

"I beg your pardon?"

"Not many dog genes left in this one if you ask me."

"What do you mean?"

"You can breed two of these together for thousands of years, honey, and you'll never get a wolf."

Duke smiled. He liked her. He liked her a lot.

She charged him eighty bucks for the consultation, hoping he'd never come back. Then she stood well back from the window and watched him drive away. Some reporter! She thought. Didn't even ask if my oven was big enough to crockpot a teenager!

We went to our Post as Pocketville attended a double funeral. Figured we best be together until the pansies got their peddles. Besides that, we had no where else to go and no energy to do it. But we did it anyway.

Our fence was heaped in a twisted pile by the road like a fishnet. Poles dipped in concrete pudding pointed all over like drunken artillery mortars.

A blue sky surprised us because they said rain. We stood, us three in our parking lot and looked over at the crater where the TV House used to be.

"So you really think he's in there?" I asked Webb.

"You tell me?"

"He'd be stinking by know," Beans always seemed to know. "And there's no animals gnawing or circling the carcass. Wherever he's at," Beans did a circle, "he's not around here."

We inhaled the spring air.

"Good chance the winter storms are done," I said.

"Good chance," Webb said, turning and sniffing. "Fish crap." He looked at his tank.

We turned. It did stink.

"How long's it been?" Beans asked.

"A few weeks," I said, looking at our prisoner tank.

"He should work off his time," Beans said. "Prisoner transfer. Give him a tooth brush and some ammonia and bleach and let him go to work. It was his idea to take the tank you know."

"I recall that being my idea," Webb said.

"Who cares?" Beans said. "Let's just get him in daylight and watch his eyes blister!"

We turned back to the VFW. We agreed to wait until the funeral was over and put the kid to work under the cover of darkness.

Webb broke the seal on the good and tank and we watched him prepare it to receive the prisoner.

Me and Beans stood watch.

Cars came and went.

"It stinks," Beans said.

"Dead fish," I said, pointing to the tank that Webb was in.

"Not that," Beans said. "Worse," he walked to the prisoner tank. "Is he alive or dead?" Beans asked.

I shrugged my shoulders. "Didn't Ned say he was alive?"

"That was days ago. I think he's dead. Smell it," he thumbed. "He's dead. You can't fake rot."

Deep Pockets drove up and turned in as me and Beans were smelling the tank. He got out and walked to us before we could lead him away.

"What stinks?" he asked.

"Where?" Beans asked.

"Around here!"

"Webb thinks its cats in this one, dead fish in that one," I said.

Deep Pockets walked over to Webb's tank and knocked on it with his knuckles, making absolutely no sound whatsoever. "Webb!" he yelled.

We walked up behind him.

"Webb!" Deep Pockets yelled louder.

"How's our thief doing?" Beans asked.

"Still sleeping it off," Deep Pockets said. "Fine with us. Gives us more time to get our numbers straight before charging him. Get it? Charging him. Ching ching!"

"Nice," I said, turning away and looking at Sherman County Prison. I admired that kid. He could rat at anytime and he's gumptioning it out!

Webb poked his head out of the fish tank like a groundhog. "What?"

Chief needs your numbers. You got more tanks than any other person in Michigan so that makes you an expert. What's the butcher's bill?"

"You mean the damage?" Webb asked.

"Ya. Chief is tallying the total for Duke Dungy."

"What's it up too?"

"Oh. It's getting pretty high."

Webb looked around. "It's muddy inside and out. Wiring's okay. Engine injectors are fouled. It happens when they go swimming without a snorkel. How's five hundred sound?"

Deep Pockets looked around and stepped closer. "Is that it? I mean, who will fix it for that?"

"Me."

"How long will it take?"

"Doesn't really matter. A week if I go slow."

"Well," Deep Pockets toed the mud. "Chief would kinda like it higher. You know, the damage bill and stuff."

"How much higher?"

"You know. Fair market replacement."

"Did he give a number," I asked, tired of ying yang because it wasn't my stuff.

"Chief was thinking fifty grand."

"Really?" Webb asked.

"Does that sound too high? Chief thought it sounded about right."

"Right for what?" Beans asked.

"Oh, you know. Restitution, paperwork, filing charges, clerk fees, court time. It's really stacking pretty high. Duke wants the full number tally on the damage path for next issue."

"What is it up too?" I asked.

"We're not final yet."

"Well tell us your not final number."

"About two and a half million," Deep Pockets said. "Chief wants Red dead if he ever gets out of bed."

"Fifty grand it is!" Webb said. "I can buy twenty five more with that."

"Great!" Deep Pockets said, scratching the number on a form and handing the clipboard up the Webb. "Sign the bottom. I'll get this right back to Chief. Maybe he'll add in some air freshener!" he said, taking the signed paper from Webb and making it back to his car, walking wide around the stink of the other tank. He gave us a thumbs-up as he closed his cruiser door.

Webb sniffed, looked concerned and climbed down. He walked to the prisoner tank and smelled deep. "That's not good," he said. "I think we got us a dead one!"

"What'd Ned expect?" Beans said. "We filled him with holes!"

"We gotta pop the top," I said.

"No way!" Webb said. "We'll just pack it with lime."

"Pop the top, Webb." I said. "Just because flesh is rotting doesn't make a man dead."

Webb looked at Beans.

Beans glanced around and nodded.

Webb went home, got his welder and came back.

I backed up my truck and Webb sparked his welder, shooting lightning at his custom seal.

The lid opened and stench rose ten fold. Beans was on top and dropped into the hole, racking a .45 into the chamber as he did so. Once a South Pacific Marine, always one.

I looked at Webb who shrugged it off. If we didn't know better, it looked like Beans enjoyed the opportunity.

"We got us a live one. But not by much." Beans said, poking his head out.

"What now?" Webb asked. "Should I pickle it? Open her back up in a couple of years?"

"Please help me," the boy asked from deep inside the tank. Not yelling or even in a whisper. Just a plead. Nothing more.

Webb hunched his shoulders.

I climbed into my flatbed.

Beans got out and he and Webb reached down and took hold of the prisoner.

And paint us purple and put us to bed if we didn't just flop that kid out of the tank and into my truck bed in broad daylight!

Beans slammed the lid down and re-glued it with liquid metal and I drove the kid to the back V.F.W. door where me and Beans hobbled the boy off the truck and inside our post.

And darn! Was that kid ever gritting her down. Blinded by sunlight. Near deaf by bombs. Burn scarred skin, half bald and thirty pounds low. But he gutted it. Me and Beans nodded to each other, admiring sand.

The last thing we had to do was worry about him running off. Let's just say the critters in his leg below the knee were running the show now. We had ecosystem!

We put him on the card table where Ned fixed Webb's eye a couple of weeks ago and the boy looked at us, squint-eyed.

"Can you turn the lights off, please?" he asked.

We did. I liked the kid. What was left of him. I didn't like the part of him that had gangrene.

No soldier likes gangrene. But yet it's the stuff that always ends up on the diner table.

"Where Ned when you need him?" I asked.

"You know if you mix it with Spam its doable," Beans said.

"Whose Ned?" the lad asked, totally out of steam.

"The Doctor. He's taken off hundreds of legs," Webb said, looking at me. "Arms too!" he smiled.

"Can you get him?"

"He's the one you shot, numbnuts," Beans said. "We can get you a normal doctor. All you have to do is say so. Of course then you would lose the war."

"I want Ned. He's the Captain. He'll do," the teenager said. "No hospitals. No reports. No surrender."

"You shot Ned dead," I said.

"He's really dead?"

"Oops for you." Webb said.

"Shooting your doctor," Beans said. "You just might be stupid enough to be put in charge of dumb!"

The boy closed his eyes. "It can't be that hard," he said. "It's mostly rotted anyways. Mostly."

Beans looked at me. "We're you awake when they took off your arm, Lefty?"

"The masher took off most of it, but they still had to spoon out some potato. I was in and out."

"What now?" Webb asked.

"We lock the doors," Beans said. "It's not that hard if you're the one holding the knife," he pulled out his K-Bar.

Webb flip flame on his lighter. "Burning off the bad germs," he said to the boy.

The boy turned and looked at me after I locked the door. Then he looked at Webb and Beans. "Sit me up for a minute, please."

We did.

He looked at us, as his elbows struggled to hold weight. "If I don't make it," he blinked. "I want you to know I'm sorry for what I did to you and your friends."

We looked at him.

"I'm the one who shot Wendell," he said.

We lowered him to his back.

"Mighty white of you, Blackie," Beans said.

I lifted one of his arms and dropped it. It thumped.

"Let's cut it while he's out," Webb said. "It's always easier when they're out."

"He's been swimming in his stink for weeks. If we cut him we kill him," I said. "We gotta clean him first."

We looked around. Windows were closed and doors were locked. We turned the lights back on, keeping a rag over the kid's face and opened up a cupboard that Ned stocked after the whole thing started going south.

I pulled down two industrial size bottles. "Betadine™," I read. "The #1 Brand Hospital Antiseptic." I handed it to Webb.

"We got septic all right," Beans said.

"Kills Germs Promptly in Minor cuts, scrapes and burns," Webb read.

"Perfect!" Beans said. "He's got all three."

"He's not strong enough to scream." I said. "That's good and bad."

We looked at the surveillance monitors and saw an empty lot but for Webb's tanks.

We took towels from under the sink and put them on the table.

I held my arm to Beans. "Can you roll up my sleeve?"

31

EXPLOSION!

Duke Dungy slouched down in his car seat as Berta finished work and walked home. He ducked lower when she stopped to scrap dog dirt off her boot. He looked at his watch. It had been dark for an hour.

He didn't like the idea of going into the clinic, but needed to verify the blueprints of the place. A pet crematorium was in the original drawings and if it was still there, he needed a sample of ash for DNA analysis.

Then headlights started up over at her house at the north end, just over the dark hill. Out came her little Toyota truck and Duke dropped below the dash, waited a few moments, then pulled out behind her.

He needed to get inside the clinic. That is why he had come. But he was a reporter by nature and was rather whimsical when it came to following a plan. Besides, she was a big girl and getting manhandled by a woman like her didn't look like a tinker toy tryout.

Keeping his lights off, he drove south by east until he saw her brakes go on at the VFW Post. He turned off road, stopped, snapped on a 400mm night vision lens on his Nikon and started running. Ahead was Berta at the VFW!

Berta was all business as she pulled up and stopped beside the gutted Sherman tank. Walking to the back of her truck, she picked up a five gallon bucket and rested it on the tank. Then she hoisted her body up onto the tank and kicked at the front slide until she jammed it open. In a fluid movement, she stepped above the hatch, swung the bucket over, pulled off the lid and poured a thick liquid into the tank.

A combination of gas and dish detergent splashed off the sides of the slide and across the tank, but most went inside.

She threw the bucket aside and got back down, in a controlled fall, rolled once and bounced back to her feet.

Dungy, crouched at the side of the fence debris pile, snapping off as many photos as he could as his other hand held the pop up flash down.

He thought he had a good one when she tumbled because he saw the white of a slip below a blue jean skirt. It would balance well with the white bucket and her truck.

Then his eyes retracted as a flare lit the yard in red light as it arched toward the tank, erupting the machine into flame.

Soon the gelatin, dripped into the interior of the tank and fire of igniting gas shot out from the slide like a half way descent flamethrower.

Dungy ejected the full photo cartridge and slammed in an empty one as the fire reached 100 feet, showing up the entire compound in an array of flame. It's higher than the pancake woman's house! He thought.

Then the truck fled the scene and Dungy sprinted back for his car, knowing his tracks were dangerously close the crime scene. He saw premeditations of Murder One for the first time in his life, even though he didn't know why murder had come into his head.

Panting, he fobbled his keys as Berta's headlights appeared and he reached to get them.

Berta's truck blew by him.

He rose from beneath the dashboard and looked out his back window. If her brake lights went on he was in trouble. And she would kill him or die trying.

Legs weak. Fingers sloppy and stiff in sweat. Heart in his throat. Guts floating in a liquid lead stomach he knew she would crush him.

Duke Dungy inhaled deep and hard. Breathing for his life, he got his story! He saw evil and its name was Berta!

Death Doctor to the fingerless, young man, Splinter.

Carcass cremator of the Jones killer, Cell.

Incinerator of the a tank in the dead of night. A tank that might even be the home of a missing teenager! Unlikely, but possible. Why had that come into his mind?

Duke knew where Berta was going know. Out to kill her lover's offspring and distance herself from the teenagers for good!

Duke started his car on its first go. His mind programmed the fastest way to Five County Hospital. He put the car in gear and reached for his phone.

Berta stood out his driver's side window and his hand went slippery on the wheel. She raised and pointed a gun at him and he screamed.

Beans rewound the monitor and we saw a big woman do her thing in slow motion.

"Wow," Beans said, holding Pal's rotten, dripping leg by its ankle with his free hand. "She was trying to kill our prisoner." He turned to Webb and me. "War. The gift that keeps on giving."

I lifted my hand, opened palmed above my head, wishing I had both to better show my exasperation to heaven.

"We gotta wipe up the blood. Deep Pockets are coming and they're all going to do a Rain Dance right here in triage!"

"What are we going to do with him?" I asked, pointing to the kid. "We can't really send him packing."

"How's the big woman involved?" Webb asked.

"Who cares!" I said, snapping my fingers at the kid's nose, trying to wake him.

"You gotta slap him!" Webb said, he had a dozen kitchen towels out, absorbing blood. "Do something with the leg, Beans."

Beans walked to the fridge.

"Not there. I don't want gangrene beer!" Webb pleaded, which didn't make much sense because he wasn't a drinker. Maybe it's never too late to change.

Beans opened the freezer above and jammed it inside. Closing the door, he wiped blood off the handle with his shirt.

Webb opened the door below the sink and stuffed in the bloody towels.

I took our last two clean ones and did a once over on the floor and table.

Sirens came closer.

"What now?" Webb asked.

From inside our VFW we felt the heat from the tank. Beans smelled. "Soap gas," he said. "If it's not broke, don't fix it."

"They're coming!" Webb said. Sirens grew louder.

"Attic!" Beans said.

"He's dead weight," I yelled. "You want to winch him up?"

"Let's chuck him out back!"

"Too cold."

Spotlights beamed across our place. Webb exhaled. "It's over," he said.

Beans stood up. "Well then let's go out and meet them and lock the door behind us."

We looked at the kid on our mildew couch. He was asleep below our plexiglass window on the other side of our table. Face pale from blood loss, dehydration and malnutrition; we knew he was more dead than alive. And the fact that we just cut his leg off wouldn't go over real well. Unless they got wind that it was us who shot him up in the first place.

By the look of the cop cars pouring in, we knew it was the Alamo for us.

"Get the tape." I pointed to our monitors.

Beans took it from where it was locked behind cupboards.

Webb had the door open and smoke poured into our building.

Black smoke billowed above the orange, chemical blaze.

We walked out into the night and stood next to the flame for warmth. Beans held his hands out to it.

Cops roared in, sirens wailing.

Wendell waved both arms as if guiding a plane to a landing.

Seeing the three of us, they stopped and were wary, knowing we had guns around. But with our hands out, they came in front of their lights.

"We saw the killer!" Webb yelled and I hoped he wouldn't say much more. Too much is a bad thing. Liars like it simple.

I held up the tape. "We caught her on film!" I said.

State Police troopers, a Highway Patrol and three County Sheriff Deputies looked at the Pocketville City Police Officer.

Deep Pockets stepped forward and took our surveillance tape and placed it into a plastic bag and zipped it up. "It's some woman," I said. "Some big woman."

The cops looked at each other. Deep Pockets spoke into his shoulder mic. The others stepped up to the fire. Being a clear night, it was right nippy.

"What happening this month around here?," one asked Beans.

Beans looked at me and nodded.

"March has come." I said to them. "It's the best month of the year. March is when Adolph Hitler froze his quarter million pets on the Russian Front!"

The cops looked at us.

"March turned the tide," I said.

"What do you do here? Live here?" one asked.

"Cards," Webb said.

"Well you men are killing us in paper work!" another said. Others nodded. A gust from the north blew in and opened coats, sending chills.

"Mind if we go inside for the paperwork?" a deputy asked. "Never been in your place."

Webb stepped forward then stopped. He didn't look too guilty.

"What do you do in there?"

"Poker," I said. "It's not the game. It's the calm."

"Texas Hold'em?"

"No. We're Michigan men," I said. "Five Card Stud."

Beans, Webb and I looked at the men in uniform and we started for the door. Webb took out the keys and bobbled them a bit and for a moment, I thought he had an idea. But he looked back at me, frowned and said nothing.

I knew Beans had a .45 still tucked away behind his belt, but it somehow seemed small and far away.

Then their command radios in their cars and on their shoulders started lighting up and quite a stir seemed to happening up the road.

Shouts drifted down to us from over a hundred yards away. They were not the noises of chance or surprise. They were the shouts of war, battle, ruin and death.

I looked at Webb and his head was down.

Beans was looking up the road. Someone up there was speaking his language.

Half the cops turned away. The others stepped onto our ramp, leading to our red, white and blue front door.

I was trying to think of some fancy lying. But I was tired. Even at my best its hard to argue away a dying, one-legged teenager on the couch.

Webb unlocked the door and we let them in. I turned on the lights and looked up the long checked floor of the hallway. Pieces of potato were still along it, as well as gravel that had been spit in by the truck. It was there if one wanted to take a close look.

We all three moped to our kitchen and to where the legless boy was asleep on the couch. We looked at each other one last time before we rounded the corner and saw the cops following along, silver clipboards in hand. Pens clicked in anticipation.

"Battles and witches," Webb said.

"Battles and witches," Beans added.

"What's that?" a cop asked.

"Long story. Long month. Long war," I said and looked at the empty couch.

The boy had gotten out of sight.

I knew I liked that kid.

Beans grunted. Blackie was one to keep on eye on, that's for sure.

Webb smiled and opened the refrigerator. "Any of you men want a Pabst?"

They declined.

I didn't. A beer sounded good.

32

"We Liked That Kid"

The boy crawled back inside the back door after the cops left. It was dark and cold in the back hallway floor and he pulled his torso along the tile, dragging his nub, leaving an ooze trail

Two hours had passed. The cops were gone and the fire was out.

We three sat under our light and dealt cards. Beans had us down a half dozen or so teeth. We played out our hand, listening to the boy crawl closer.

He made it into our room and Webb took two cards and tossed in a tooth.

Pal looked up at us from the floor and pulled his good leg under him and pushed himself towards the sofa. Looking up at the window, he seemed to see paintball residue.

It had been cleaned but he saw it nevertheless.

Pal took hold of the armrest, grunted and got himself seated on the couch as the room circled around his head.

For an hour he watched us as he laid there.

With only two pair, I called Beans and won ten teeth on a single bet. He counted them out, each thumping on the table, then he rolled them into my nest.

"On my way now, Beans. I've come to get what was mine."

For the next hour or so, it was even, then someone knocked at our door and I looked around.

The boy sat up and looked scared.

They all nodded to me as if the three of them were stitched to bedpans.

I sat still.

"You gonna get the door, Lefty?" Beans asked, "Or you gonna sit there and whiffle your sniffle?" His cheeks had a good sag and were chalky white.

I grunted as I stood, for it was after ten and hours since my last nap. I shuffled, wishing I had my cane.

"Having a good night, Lefty?" Deep Pockets asked, taking off his hat after he stepped in.

"A little late to be out collecting from the poor," I said.

"Yes. Yes it is," he said. "But can you pass it along to your comrades that the woman on the tape, was the one that used to work at the animal clinic up the road."

"Used to?"

"She killed the comatose kid before she was shot and killed by law enforcement." He looked around. Then put his hat back on. "I knew you men hadn't had much peace around here so Chief sent me down straight away. We thought we'd let you know that is seems like she had a little beef with America and somehow got those punks to do some crazy stuff. But it's over now so you fella's can rest in peace. We sorry you men got blindsided and we're just glad none of you got hurt."

"Thank you officer. I'll let the men know." I said and opened the door for him to exit.

I watched him drive off. I was halfway back down the hallway before I heard the airshock release and knew the door had closed without latching.

I try never to lock a door. It brings the devil up from the depths and makes your bones old with the cancer of fear.

I made it back to the table and looked at the three men. Nub had made it into Wendell's chair and Webb had dealt him in. Of course he still dealt in Ned.

"She's dead," I said.

No surprise there.

Nub took up his cards, hands shaking against each other as he did so. He dropped one to the floor and I reached down and picked it up for him.

I saw Webb holding spades. Lots of them. Enough to dig graves for all of us and then some.

We finished up some strong hands until April came and the thaw. Nub shakes a bit more than usual for someone his age. His face always seems to sweat when he sits for more than an hour or so. But he sits anyways. He sleeps off his time on the couch and we consensus that hope will come for him.

After the thaw he asked us something for the first time. "How do I get teeth?" he looked at us.

Beans looked at Webb then me."What?" Beans asked.

I shook my head.

Webb looked at the boy then at me. "The frost is out of the ground." He said. "It's time."

"Time for what?" Nub asked.

"Time for you to get some poker chips." Beans said and we all made it outside and got in my truck.

We drove with the windows down. Life was in the air once again and trees were cloaked in green as we traveled north. Going from pavement, to gravel then turning onto two-tracks weaved north until the branches scraped the sides of my truck and twigs scratched at our faces inside open windows.

Ned's cabin appeared.

Beans got out and stretched. Webb too.

Nub followed, going slow, his crutches sinking into moss and goo.

Webb opened Ned's unlocked door and waved the kid in.

Nub entered.

I liked that kid. Brave.

The blast of death hit him hard but he held ground. None of us had much back up.

Ned was on his rocker, long dead and decayed. Around the table he had dealt out five hands of cards. All were face down, as were the dealers. We looked at each hand.

Where Wendell sat rested a royal flush in clubs.

Webb had been dealt the same in hearts.

Beans had one in diamonds.

I had a six of clubs. Nine of diamonds. Two and spades four of spades and a seven in hearts. "He stacked the deck," I said.

Webb and Beans smirked at this.

I didn't.

Nub either.

Ned's cards were face down.

Beans turned Ned's cards face up. Underneath them was his thin silver dollar and his Leatherman™ utility knife opened to needle nose pliers burned black with carbon.

"What was he dealt?" Webb asked

"Royal Flush. Spades!" Beans said.

We leaned in to see them and then we sat and Webb kicked Wendell's chair out for Nub, who sat last.

I gathered the cards. Nub sat by Ned, feeling awkward with the corpse. Mice had had their way with him but his mouth still had its grin.

Beans took out a large handful of gold teeth and let them pour out the bottom of his grip to the table where they sang out in a nice, expensive ring.

Webb unloaded about the same amount in front of him.

I was low. Holding only thirteen. It had been a rough month for me.

Nub looked at us. "What about me?" he asked.

Beans nodded to for him to look at Ned. "Not all our teeth have come from dead Nazis," he said.

Webb dealt.

We all pulled in our cards.

Nub still had the shakes.

"Ante up, Nub," Beans said. "You going to pull out some gold teeth or reminisce about playing kick the can?"

We sat our cards in order and then looked over them at the boy, whose hand shook a bit as he took up the pliers.

We liked that kid.

THE END

www.ingramcontent.com/pod-product-compliance
Lightning Source LLC
Chambersburg PA
CBHW061428040426
42450CB00007B/948